Frederic W. H. Myers

The S
of

The Secularization of the Soul

Psychical Research
in Modern Britain

John J. Cerullo

A Publication of the
Institute for the Study of Human Issues
Philadelphia

Manufactured in the United States of America

Frontispiece courtesy of Mary Evans/Society for
Psychical Research, London

Library of Congress Cataloging in Publication Data

Cerullo, John James, 1949–
    The secularization of the soul.

    Bibliography: p.
    Includes index.
    1. Psychical research—Great Britain—History.
    2. Society for Psychical Research (London, England)—
History.   I. Title.
    BF1028.5.G7C47   133.8'01   81-13322
    ISBN 0-89727-028-2   AACR2

For information, write:

Director of Publications
ISHI
3401 Market St.
Philadelphia, Pennsylvania 19104
U.S.A.

To my parents,
Leonard and Marion Cerullo

Contents

Acknowledgments

This study could not have been completed without the assistance of many people. The cooperation I received at the Society for Psychical Research in London was particularly important. I would like to thank specifically Nicholas Clarke-Lowes, Hugh Pincott, Leslie Price, and especially Eleanor O'Keeffe and Renée Haynes for their help. I am grateful also to Laura Dale of the American Society for Psychical Research, who was kind enough to read and criticize the manuscript. Seymour Mauskopf and R. Laurence Moore offered expert guidance when the project was in its formative stage, as did Fraser Nicol. The study certainly owes a great deal to two gentlemen I have not met: Alan Gauld and Frank Miller Turner. I would also like to note the contribution of Michael and Jane Hogan, not only for reading and criticizing this manuscript but for years of friendship and support.

Personnel at the University of Pennsylvania were, of course, invaluable. The research that led to this book was funded by the History Department's award of a Lingelbach Fellowship. Dan Hirschberg of the History Department and Samuel Klausner of the Sociology Department were extremely helpful throughout the entire period of research and writing.

Irma Flaim's help at a particularly critical juncture is most warmly appreciated. In addition, I am profoundly grateful to the publications staff at the Institute for the Study of Human Issues, especially my editor Peggy Gordon. I will not soon forget her confidence in, and patience with, a sometimes jittery first-time author.

Finally, I would like to acknowledge in a special way the contributions of Jack Reece, also of the University of Pennsylvania. His criticisms and encouragement have been equally important to me over the years, and this study could never have been imagined without him.

Introduction

The term "psychical research" conjures up visions of ghosts and apparitions, clairvoyance and thought transference, occult arcana and assorted things that go bump in the night. Those are indeed the sorts of phenomena psychical researchers have investigated. But the objective truth or falsity of claims they have made regarding such matters—still controversial among scientists—is completely outside the scope of this work. Here I have chosen to address the attraction the entire enterprise held for intellectuals and nonintellectuals alike at a certain juncture in the evolution of a certain society. For the story of psychical research is really the story of people trying to assemble a delineation of human selfhood amidst what they saw as the most challenging circumstances: the erosion of a tradition that could not be sustained, by new formulations that could not be tolerated.

It is no accident that psychical research emerged in Britain and was practiced most earnestly there and in the United States. Those cultures encompassed religious belief systems—Protestant versions of Christianity—in such a way as to make peculiar demands on the individual. While those belief systems functioned, he could understand his own selfhood ultimately in terms of the soul. He could rest assured that a part of him was ineffable, unique, immortal if nourished properly by the type of life he led in this world. But those systems were also peculiarly vulnerable to secularizing forces—indeed, they almost invited them—that would challenge not just the strength of ecclesiastical institutions but the status of religious ideas. During the nineteenth and early twentieth centuries, scientists attempted to move into the cultural territory vacated by religion. But science's alternative view of selfhood (or, perhaps, its failure to provide any singular or cogent view of selfhood) was disquieting. First in Spiritualism and then in psychical research, what we see is an attempt to come to terms with scientific thought while retaining the understanding of the self that religious tradition had transmitted. It was not an easy synthesis to accomplish in a cultural climate characterized in many quarters by the most militant scientism.

In that climate, the psychical researchers produced something genuinely startling. Forced by the logic of their position to recast the concept of the soul into a form more palatable to scientists, they came up with a formulation I call "the secular soul." It was a vision of selfhood that whittled down the Western religious sensibility to its barest essence and, in doing so, magnified its most intoxicating assertion. It was a vision of the self that incorporated what had been the supernatural qualities of the soul into the worldly persona itself, with the vitalism religion would truly unleash only after death operational in the here and now. It was a vision of protean man.

That vision came closer to achieving mainstream status within the new psychological profession than is generally recognized. It also exerted a very real popular appeal. Perhaps the most intriguing aspect of the story of psychical research is the manner in which its statement on selfhood appears to have answered the needs of people caught in subtle offshoots of that great industrialization/urbanization complex of interlocking social changes we associate with modernity in the West. The people who embraced it seem to have felt that concomitant sociocultural processes—the bureaucratization, routinization, and rationalization of social life—threatened their sense of self in the most unexpected ways. Even within the ranks of that great, triumphant, enormously accomplished and confident bourgeoisie of Victorian and Edwardian Britain, there were doubts about the ability of modern culture to satisfy the most elementary requirement of any culture. For some, it was psychical research that provided what their own lifestyle could not. The secular soul was refuge and remedy.

That remedy, however, could not be accommodated easily. Modern British social life demanded not a protean but a functional view of the self. In the end, the psychical researchers' vision would be eclipsed by one from which rationales for social order could more easily be extracted. That was the version of Sigmund Freud.

With the appearance of Freudian thought, psychical research, and all that it represented, met its most formidable and effective antagonist. It was not that Freud himself waged war on it (although, in essays like "The Uncanny," he explicitly placed subconscious pathologies where psychical researchers had sketched the secular soul). Rather, it was that his ideas provided models of the self that could serve the exigencies of modern social organization better than those of psychical research. He was "therapeutic" where they were dysfunctional. He was, in the most real sense, the safer alternative for society as it was then constituted. From about the 1920s on, psychical research was forced from center stage onto the wings of the psychological profession. It remains there today, still practiced if usually unheeded.

Why, it might be asked, should we interest ourselves in this matter? If, as has been stated, it is primarily the ideas represented by psychical research that this study seeks to clarify, what possible connection can they now have with our own lives, marginal as those ideas are in intellectual officialdom? There are a variety of answers. To those interested in religion, it might be useful to see what was rendered when serious accommodation with a scientific world view was attempted in the past: a reduction of the religious sensibility to its most profoundly invigorating kernel. To those interested in psychology, it might be useful to note the direction that field once could have taken (there are in psychical research substantive foreshadowings of contemporary post-Freudianism). But it is my contention that there is an intrinsic interest in the story of psychical research that reaches beyond academic specialities, even beyond the circumscribed concerns of professional intellectuals.

We are now, perhaps more than ever, concerned with the self. As our technologies provide more and more leisure time, we probe it, experiment with it, brood about it to a degree that shocks some, amuses others. In the final analysis, what we see in psychical research is commitment to the idea that whatever the self is, it is not to be feared. Those endorsing that notion, in whatever profession or whatever life-style, will find compatriots here. Those committed to alternative per-spectives can find sobering reminders that in the past their opponents have appeared in the unlikeliest places. This study does not attempt to reinforce either reflex. It merely, I hope, touches the nerve.

It is submitted, then, not as polemic but as a simple exercise in the history of ideas. Yet the reader will notice at once that it has not been assembled as most intellectual histories are. Sociological theory; institutional analysis; biography; considerations of scientific, religious, and psychological thought; treatments of popular social movements; even plainly metahistorical musings—all have their place in this story. An explanation of what is admittedly a fairly unusual approach to an old and venerable branch of historical investigation is therefore in order.

For some years now, historians in all fields have been reappraising long-held assumptions about the methods and purpose of their work. Older models of professional excellence in conceptualization and re-search design have been held to rest on flawed notions of explanatory adequacy, personal objectivity, or the very value of historical inquiry. Contemporary scholars tend to speak contemptuously of what is termed "traditional intellectual history," which generally involved examining ideas held by some celebrated intellectual or school of intellectuals by tracing those ideas' pedigrees back to previous intellectuals' views. This sort of thing has been decried as representing the assumptions that consequential ideas are the playthings of professional ideamongers alone, that intellectuals live and work in a rarefied atmosphere in-habited only by other intellectuals, neither touched by nor touching the concerns of mass society. Such assumptions, it was held, were demonstrably false and bespoke a suspiciously undemocratic fixation on "high culture" or the activities of intellectual elites. Work undertaken along those lines failed to make the vital connection between ideas and the day-to-day lives of the masses, an altogether more wholesome concern, it was said, for historians of ideas to address.

And so we addressed it. But there were no precedents to guide us, no methodological models to emulate. The closest thing we could find to guidelines came from what is called "the sociology of knowledge." In that area of scholarship, we found ideas viewed not in terms of anyone's self-contained intellectual labor, not even in terms of the "influence" exerted by those who had previously labored, but as "reflections" of the general social climate surrounding the thinker. Ideas, to some scholars, became what Marx called the "superstructure" of social life: epiphenomena of material "interests" generated in the far more important world or production, profit, and power (whether those expressing them recognized it or not). Other scholars, more interested in change than in the status quo, tried to treat ideas as one among many "variables" affecting social change; tried to fit them into overall diagrams of the determinants of change; tried most assiduously to figure out precisely what their real "weight" in processes of change might be—the better to predict, promote, or perhaps master it.

The study you are about to read was molded in part by misgivings concerning both the traditional and the modern practice of intellectual history. In my opinion, ideas most certainly do not exist in a vacuum, and unless they are related to larger currents than those found within the ranks of the intelligentsia, either in formation or in consequence, they have been deprived by the historian of their very life-support systems. At the same time, it is very difficult to breathe any life into ideas of the past when the historian's focus is completely on the social processes surrounding them. Ideas, in that design, tend to become quaint accoutrements to bygone sociological mechanics.

I wanted the ideas discussed in this study to die neither of suffocation nor neglect. I wanted them to stay paramount. And I found that in order to keep them paramount, to keep them in the bold relief I felt they merited, I was compelled to place them against a variety of backdrops. Hence the array of analytical zones into which this study moves and the array of methods it employs. I cannot offer any novel methodological conceptualization into which this work can be fit. I can only advise that it be read, quite simply, as a story. The story is set in a broadly sketched social context. It has a large cast of characters: people in different social locations, in different times, confronting different sorts of pressures. But its focus is the ideas those people held on a certain subject, and treatments of social processes are intended to highlight and clarify the ideas, not vice versa. It is my opinion that those ideas are indeed interesting and important in and of themselves, because they deal with the most elemental questions we have always had to face and always will. They deal with the nature of the self.

*The Secularization
of the Soul*

Chapter One

Secularization and the Concept of Noumenal Selfhood in Modern Protestant Cultures

THE THEOLOGICAL ISSUE

Psychical research was officially born in Britain in the late nineteenth century. It was at first almost entirely a British and American affair, a product of the Anglo-American Protestant milieu. In fact, its coming reflected an acute intellectual dilemma experienced by a variety of people in those environments. That dilemma involved their religious sensibilities. It was a dilemma—rather, a challenge—that participants in a Protestant Christian culture during the modern era could experience viscerally. For it is in modern Protestant cultures that people have actually found themselves intellectually committed simultaneously to a religious tradition and to the process of secularization. In modern Protestant cultures, affirmation of one can actually imply affirmation of the other. Individuals who believe so have been forced to confront the dizzying, or exhilarating, task of reconciling the two.

The term "secularization" connotes the removal of religious ideas and institutions from positions of great or even coercive influence in politics, economics, jurisprudence, community organization, family life, and intellectual activity.[1] That gradual erasure is often held to constitute a key motif in the evolution of Western civilization.[2] Yet the divestiture of ecclesiastical suasions from the world is seen fairly unambiguously as a threat to personal religiosity only within one of the two great branches of Christianity. The fundamental theological postulates of Catholicism and Protestantism actually provide contrasting understandings of personal religiosity and, consequently, grounds for divergent interpretations of secularization.

Theologically, the Catholic God is usually described as a relatively immanent God, one whose manifestations directly or indirectly pervade all aspects of creation.[3] His ongoing presence in the world, realized most fully in the Incarnation and carried forward by the works of the Holy Spirit, suffuses the total environment of man with sacrality. In doctrine, the Church is charged with the task of mediating this sacred presence to men, interpreting and relating it to their experience in such a manner as to expand the spiritual quality of their existence.

Under that theological scheme, personal religiosity is for the most part nurtured and contained within the institutional matrix of the Roman Church itself. It is usually felt to involve a relatively intense appreciation of the world's inherently numinous character, "mystified," as it were, by the indwelling Godhead of Catholic theology.[4] A specifically Catholic religious consciousness is transmitted only by the Church (through the dissemination of her standardized catechism by clerical functionaries) and is expressed only in or with the Church (through devotional rites and sacramental observances conducted in an institutional setting or by institutional representatives). It thus follows that the personal religiosity of Catholics is best demonstrated by the closeness of their affiliation with the Church, the level of their involvement in and endorsement of her institutional activities.

Therefore, in the Catholic case any empirical decline in the Church's ability to mobilize social support has been understood to indicate a decline in the religiosity of Catholics. That dual decline is what is clearly meant by "secularization." The logical culmination of this process would be a society emptied of both Catholicism's institutional apparatus and the particular religious sensibility that goes with it. This can be deplored or applauded, depending on whether or not Catholicism's version of religious life (with its obeisance before the Church and acknowledgment of the world's relatively "enchanted" character) is deemed desirable. In either event, it is rather clearly understood.[5]

But the Catholic assessment of secularization, in its neat identification of the Church's institutional authority with the personal religiosity of believers, is wholly inappropriate to the Protestant context. Protestantism's fundamental theological divergence from Catholicism translates into entirely different brands of religiosity, versions much less easily correlated to the status of religious institutions as such. As a result, the entire issue of secularization is far more complex and, perhaps, more analytically challenging in the Protestant world.

For all the doctrinal heterogeneity of the Protestant faiths, the great theological innovation from which they have all to some degree derived is customarily seen as the replacement of the immanent God of Catholicism with one more nearly resembling the transcendent one of Jewish tradition. The God described by Reformation thinkers (particularly, of course, by Calvin and those most directly influenced by him) simply will not irrupt into either the natural or social environment as directly or regularly as does that of Catholicism. The Catholic world was permeated by supernatural manifestations: miracles, saintly intercessions, even the sacraments themselves. Direct interventions by the heavenly realm were normal, expected (even invokable) features of reality in Catholic eyes. Protestantism denied most of them. The God it portrayed would not grant such "popish" boons to a mankind as utterly, frightfully fallen as Luther and Calvin believed. In the final analysis, only one undeniably supernatural event was allotted Protestant man: the devolution of God's sovereign grace.[6]

Lutheranism and Calvinism made the most extreme departures from the Catholic notion of an immanent God. Anglicanism, of course, deviated less from that notion. The Protestant faiths that eventually followed those three original ruptures with Roman Catholic tradition formed their own specific ideas of just how directly involved in the day-to-day operations of the world the divinity really was. Methodism and Unitarianism, for instance, are generally considered to present relatively transcendent Gods to believers, as does the Quaker faith. Baptist and "Fundamentalist" sects, on the other hand, present relatively immanent deities. These, however, are all understood in comparison with Catholicism, which still portrays the most immanent God in Christianity. Anglicanism and Episcopalianism remain the closest correlates in the Protestant world, but they also most definitely remain parts of that Protestant world. Over the years, they and all other Protestant faiths have had to deal with certain logical implications of their determinations of God's distance from the world.

To the degree that God is seen as transcendent, the world itself must be seen as significantly less invested with miraculous potentialities. To the degree that the intrinsic numinosity of the world is deemphasized, so too are institutionalized mediations of it. That is, as the world itself is demystified, any church loses the capacity to abet the appearance of miracles in any form on believers' behalf, or even to offer believers any means of invoking them themselves. Sometimes, this has meant narrowing the function of churchly institutions to transmission of "the Word," or God's prescriptions for the health of the soul. Excepting those Protestant faiths most closely related to Catholicism, ritualized sacramental and devotional linkages to numinous reality (the Mass, for instance) have been deemphasized in Protestantism because doctrinally that numinous reality is often simply not posited or thought to be "reachable" in the world we inhabit. In comparison to Catholicism, the scope of the sacred in the outer world is often circumscribed in Protestant thought, sometimes (especially in Calvinist-derived faiths) rather severely so.

Sometimes there has been instead a relatively compressed conferral of ontological status on man alone. Sometimes he and only he, among all the entities of creation and all the components of the universe, is held to be in any sense touched with the miraculous. Under theological regimens constructed along those lines, the soul cannot be fortified by sacramental or institutional connections with any "outer" numinosity because there is no such "outer" numinosity (save God himself, far removed from this world). Rather, numinosity resides within man. The human soul is the only real repository of sacrality in this world, and while the Word can offer guidelines for the soul's well-being, no church can offer institutionally mediated nutrients.[7]

The upshot of this is that, again excepting primarily Anglicanism, Protestant versions of religiosity are often less "contained," doctrinally, within the formal, institutional settings of the church than is that of Catholicism. There has been less of a tendency among Protestant theologians to think of the soul's health in terms of what transpires with or through the Church than among Catholics. Instead, there has been more of a tendency to think of it in terms of what transpires among men, in the social world. But this creates a special theological problem when the issue of secularization is raised.

In a sense, much of Protestantism is built on what Catholics would have to consider concomitant features of the secularization process. Emptying the outer world of numinosity and deemphasizing institutional mediations of it means an effective dismantling of the Catholic's spiritual vision as sustained by the Church. If the flow of secularization is demystifying and counter-ecclesiastical, as it is generally acknowledged to be, then much of Protestant thought itself can be said to contain a secularizing motif.[8] This is precisely what makes the interpretation of secularization in Protestant contexts so difficult for theologians. If secularization is understood as a continuing reduction of organized ecclesiastical influence in society and of supernatural referents in its culture, then does it imply a threat to Protestant spirituality or rather the progressive flowering of it? Given the general theological framework of Protestantism, there can be only one point of reference: the degree to which individuals continue to act upon that awesome charge, their own souls. In fact, the dominant concern of modern Protestant theology has been the implications secularization holds for that particular form of *praxis*.

Conservatives argue that the social locus of ecclesiastical institutions and the range of supernaturalism in human culture were both sufficiently delimited during the Reformation. They submit that further erosion of the latter must result in denial of the Word's status as divine revelation, while further reductions in the former impair the churches' function as transmitters of that revelation.[9] Unchecked secularization, they claim, means a withering of the soul. Liberals, on the other hand, contend that each erasure decried by the conservatives actually widens the field in which individuals can voluntarily express that personal numinosity conveyed and confirmed by the Word. They exalt both reason and independent ethical action. Their claim is that, far from representing a withering of the soul, secularization means its complete enfranchisement, and thus fulfills the original promise of the Reformation.[10] The conflict reflects divergent views of Protestant religiosity itself, of the proper sphere and nature of religious life. Conservatives tend to set the former within the churches, and to view the latter in terms of faith in the ultimate meaningfulness of the cosmos. Liberals have argued from the beginning that its sphere is the human community at large, and its expression is not some disassociated sense of awe but socially engaged ethics. While by no means unchallenged, the liberals have generally been the dominant theological force in modern times.[11] Their gamble has been that as both institutional direction and supernatural confirmations of religious faith gradually recede, Protestant man will successfully meet the challenge for which he has been historically trained. He is to act righteously without institutional coercion, to know the way without supernatural illumination. He has heard the Word. His own soul must guide.[12]

What is risked in this, obviously, is nothing less than the entire moral complexion of Protestant-built societies. If the liberal gamble has been successful, then a certain moral ethos should have reached well beyond the confines of the churches and embedded itself in the structural foundations and processes of daily life.[13] The alternative scenario, of course, yields considerably less comforting visions.[14] The outcome, finally, can only be determined by the manner in which participants in secularizing, liberal Protestant cultures have reacted to some very serious pressures.

COGNITIVE PRESSURES: THE RATIONALIZATION MOTIF

It is probably less wise to speak of any single outcome of secularization than it is to speak of a multitude of them. For in modern Protestant cultures, each individual bearing a Protestant (or Protestantized) religious sensibility has had to confront and in some way resolve the cognitive issues raised by secularization. In fact, there may be no more fundamental intellectual challenge in such individuals' lives.

Most analysts of religion would agree that characterizing a particular form of human consciousness as "religious" necessarily implies that it incorporates some nonmaterial, nontemporal dimension into its construction of meaningful reality. In any religious mind, properly speaking, the awareness of that "wholly other" dimension carries with it the demand that the individual somehow relate himself to it, somehow find the surroundings or activities that effectively express his sense of enclosure within and ultimate accountability to it. Those surroundings or activities are labeled "sacred." In or by them, the religious individual conducts worship or practices "religiosity." Be they totemic symbols, sacramental rites, or even personal experiences, sacred objects and practices constitute his linkage to numinous reality itself.[15] Some religions confer sacrality on a variety of phenomena, often natural ones. Many Protestant faiths, however, confer it in rather compressed form on man himself. In such cases, the only real linkage to the realm of "otherness" actually resides within, in the form of the soul. The believer's own being thus affords the only available conduit to the ineffable. To him, human selfhood is itself noumenal, in that within the self exists the only noumenal referent he has. His means of relating himself to the total dimension of "otherness" (encoded, perhaps, as "heaven" or even "Providence") must involve, as do those of any religious believer, appropriately reverent behavior wherever sacrality resides. Since in his case it resides within himself and other men, it is indeed logical to expect that society be to some degree his church, and the proper treatment of fellow men (and their proper treatment of him) his form of worship. Yet whatever specific moral principles are elaborated to conduct this worship, those principles issue in the first place from entirely nonmaterial categories of reality in the believer's overall cognitive apparatus. Their meaningfulness derives from the meaningfulness he can attribute to "otherness," to "sacrality," and, especially, to "the soul." If his principles are forceful, it is because on some level he takes those categories seriously.

But this is easier said than done, for his world is particularly hard on that sort of mentality. It might even be said that the cognitive reality of the soul is most imperiled precisely where it is most crucial to the entire religious world view. A substantial body of scholarly work argues that such nonmaterial categories have been seriously eroded if not eliminated as components of human consciousness in the modern West.[16] In fact, the works of Max Weber read almost like a historical obituary for concepts of nonmaterial reality, for the soul, for the good life as religion would in any way form it. As has often been observed, one of the most striking features of his analysis is its irony.

Weber felt that the behavioral norms attendant upon religious sensibilities in the West had themselves promoted what he called a "rationalization" process in society and culture. For Weber, the actual practice of religious life in the West had tended to eliminate over time a sense of the miraculous or ineffable in man's perceptions of the world by encouraging ever more purposive, calculated, goal-oriented conduct in it. In comparing Western and Eastern religious evolution, Weber claimed to have discovered that the former manifested from the beginning a subtle but tangible and historically unique subordination of mystical or "other-worldly" cognition to those ideational patterns that first imparted intelligible order to the social world and would, finally, yield mastery over nature. The social dynamic carrying this "rationalization" process forward within the religious context itself involved, in Weber's view, transitions in the quality of religious leadership and the personnel or social strata supplying it. Shifts from "exemplary" to "ethical" prophecy (understood, in Weber's ideal-typical form, as shifts from investiture of authority in an individual or small group to its embodiment in some standardized system of morality) abetted the process of rationalizing normative behavior and, hence, social organization itself. Weber found such transitions in ancient Judaism and, proceeding from it, in Christianity, with Jesus the "breakthrough" ethical prophet.[17]

Weber's description of Christianity's subsequent evolution concentrated on Protestantism, with relatively scant attention to Catholicism. He was working on a study of Catholicism near the end of his life, and it seems likely that he would have seen its "remystification" of the world as a temporarily retrograde interlude in Western religious history. It was in Protestantism that Weber found the seeds of modern rationality. The controversy over his "Protestant ethic" thesis unfortunately tends to obscure the overall picture he drew of Protestantism's role in this historical process. Whatever the specific relationship between Protestantism and modern capitalism, in Weber's view it was only part (albeit an integral part) of a much larger process of interaction between Western sociocultural environments and the religiosity of the individuals within them. His contention was that Protestantism, and especially Calvinism, provided an unintentional but enormously powerful, and in fact irrevocable, push toward a rationalized world. Modern capitalism, he felt, had to do with the rationalized pursuit of material well-being, and he attributed its origins explicitly to the unadmitted psychological need of Calvinists in particular to demonstrate membership in the elect. But in a larger sense Protestantism served to intensify the process of rationalization by promoting, both deliberately and unwittingly, the notion that the quality of our earthly lives is our own and not God's responsibility.[18]

The great irony in Weber's work, of course, lies in his claim that the rationalized society encouraged by Western religion generally and Protestantism in particular turns out to be fundamentally inimical to any genuinely religious sensibility at all, to any sense of sacrality in either public or private life. The rational frame of reference is mundane, not ineffable; empirical, not noumenal; worldly, not sacred.[19] Further, Weber saw the triumph of rationalized cognition in the entire fabric of social, political, and economic life in the modern West. The historical progression he drew from "charismatic" through "legal-rational" to "bureaucratic" structures of sociopolitical authority reflected, to him, the realization of the rationalization motif in Western history.[20] What he felt had occurred first within Western religious traditions them-selves was gradually but implacably projected outward, resulting in the transformation of society as a whole.[21] In its most focused form, he saw the rationalization motif in the scientific professions. Weber seems to have felt that a society in which such immense status could accrue to those professions was a society increasingly hostile to the retention of nonmaterial, nontemporal categories of reality in human thought. It was a society quite prepared to give up the ghost, as it were, of religious consciousness. Naturally, if numinosity were becoming a meaningless category, then the conceptualization of noumenal self-hood, with all it entailed for the conduct of social life and the organiza-tion of human personality itself, must certainly die as well. With a vision oddly similar to that of Protestant theology's conservative critics of secularization, what Weber saw was a society poised and waiting for the final annihilation of the soul.[22]

Clearly, there are a number of ways in which people holding religious ideas can, and perhaps have, come to terms with the modern world, and with modern rationality or science. Cognitively, one can hold (as did Einstein, for instance) that scientific inquiries yield not a totally denoumenalized universe but rather an increasingly unexplained one, and thus do indeed leave room for ideas of ultimate cause, pur-pose, even "otherness." Or, one can hold that the scientific understand-ing of nature is irrelevant to the religious understanding of existence, that each can be compartmentalized. For that matter, science and rationality can be ignored altogether as intellectual problems for believ-ers. Individuals can retain a religious consciousness simply by associat-ing themselves as exclusively as possible with those groups and institu-tions that uncritically reinforce it. Indeed, there are a variety of ways in which a religious sensibility can, hypothetically, survive. It is possible that in Protestant societies the idea of the soul has been preserved in all sorts of manners yet to be investigated by historians.

But American and British history record one attempt to preserve the soul that is particularly intriguing because those involved in it believed themselves to be confronting the heart of the matter. It was an effort to integrate the notion of noumenal human selfhood not into specific scientific cosmologies or interpretations of the universe but rather into that empiricist epistemology understood most broadly as "Science" itself. In that sense, it may actually have been the most direct attempt to grapple with the status of the soul in a rationalized culture. Eventually, it would almost crack the casings of the understanding of human selfhood offered by the cultures in which it matured.

This attempt was mounted by the Spiritualists and, later, by the practitioners of psychical research.

NOTES

1. See Larry Shiner's "The Concept of Secularization in Empirical Research," *Journal for the Scientific Study of Religion,* vol. 6 (Fall 1967), pp. 207–20; and Bernard Groethuysen's "Secularism" in *The Encyclopedia of the Social Sciences* (New York: Macmillan, 1934).

2. Hannah Arendt calls it simply "the separation of religion and politics," with "politics" understood as public life in the broadest sense *(Between Past and Future* [Cleveland: Meridian, 1963], p. 69). See also Eric Kahler's *Man The Measure* (New York: Pantheon, 1943) or Stringfellow Barr's *The Pilgrimage of Western Man* (Philadelphia: J. B. Lippincott, 1962). For a recent and vigorously disapproving treatment, see Jacques Ellul's *The New Demons* (New York: Seabury, 1975).

3. Peter Berger discusses Catholic theology as a continuing extension of Christianity's original departure from the idea of a radically transcendent divinity that is embodied in the Jewish religious tradition. That is, Catholic theology elaborated on the idea that God may indeed "descend" into the world or involve himself with it, as first expressed in the doctrine of the Incarnation. Hence the whole range of angels, saints, and miracles—agents or expressions of the Almighty's will in the world—with which Catholicism filled the believer's conceptualization of reality. To the degree that the divine transcendence is modified, to the degree that the divinity can or will manifest himself in the day-to-day world, the world itself is, in Catholicism,

"remystified" (*The Sacred Canopy* [New York: Doubleday, 1967], pp. 121–22).

4. Berger goes so far as to argue that "the crucial Catholic doctrine of the *analogia entis* between God and man, between heaven and earth," in a sense replicates the cosmologies of pre-Biblical religions (ibid., p. 122).

5. Gabriel Le Bras has been the single most important critic of this line of reasoning on secularization in Catholic societies. His opposition stems from his conviction that loyalty to the Church does not necessarily imply authentic personal spirituality, and that what concerned Catholics often call "dechristianization" is in fact seriously misnamed ("Déchristianisation: mot fallacieux," *Social Compass*, vol. 10, no. 6 [1963], pp. 445–52). His views have stimulated a new school of "religious sociology" that attempts to gauge the actual depth of personal religious commitment behind churchly affiliation within Catholicism. But, Vatican II notwithstanding, Le Bras and his followers diverge quite dramatically from mainstream Catholic thought on the subject (except, perhaps, in America). The general temper of orthodox Catholic views on secularization is probably best gauged simply by reading papal encyclicals, from Pius IX's *Syllabus of Errors* (1864) onward.

6. Berger, *The Sacred Canopy*, p. 112.

7. Doctrinal issues such as these, derived from different interpretations of God's transcendent nature, have contributed to the formation of reformed branches of Lutheranism and Calvinism, to the splitting of the Methodist church, and to a variety of other institutional rearrangements among the Protestant denominations.

8. Berger insists that Protestant theology and religious practice fostered intellectual predispositions that were crucial for the subsequent processes of institutional secularization in the West (*The Sacred Canopy*, p. 113).

9. The most sophisticated articulation of the conservative point of view is probably found in the works of Karl Barth, especially in his *Epistle to the Romans*, trans. Edwyn C. Hoskyns (London: Oxford University Press, 1950). Other examples are offered by proponents of "Fundamentalism" in its various forms.

10. This strain dates at least back to Schliermacher's *Addresses on Religion to its Cultured Despisers* of 1799. The Schliermachian tradition was extended into the nineteenth century by Albrecht Ritschl *(The Christian Doctrine of Justification and Reconciliation)* and by Adolf von Harnack *(History of Dogma)*. Barthian conservatism was very influential between the two world wars, as can be seen in the reevaluations of liberalism undertaken by Paul Tillich *(Systematic Theology)* and Reinhold Niebuhr *(Faith and History)*. But after the Second World War, the liberal tradition returned emphatically in the works of Diet-

claimed that the raps were attributable to the spirit of a peddler ("Mr. Splitfoot") who had been murdered in the house years before. They claimed to be in communication with the spirit by means of a code of counterraps, and insisted that the departed soul had in this manner manifested its presence quite tangibly. From this seemingly frivolous, if unusual, domestic interlude, modern Spiritualism was born.

So intense and intrusive was the curiosity of the neighbors that the girls were taken to Rochester to reside with a married sister. But the disembodied rappings continued, despite alternating exorcisms and allegations of fraud by confused Rochester clergymen. The Fox girls, a few friends, and a handful of sympathetic clerics proceeded to set up the first modern Spiritualist circle: an attempt to establish formal channels of sensory communication with actual denizens of the spirit world. This undertaking proved fascinating to unexpectedly large numbers of Rochesterites. The Fox sisters' circle attracted so much local attention that in 1849 a public demonstration of the girls' ability to communicate with spirits was given in Corinthian Hall, the city's largest public meeting house. In addition, three private investigating committees of prominent citizens looked into the matter. Each reported an inability to explain the rappings that occurred in the sisters' presence.

Newspaper coverage of these events in Rochester piqued interest elsewhere, and a series of (paid) public demonstrations throughout the East was arranged for Kate and Margaret by another sister, Leah. Over the next two years the girls added to their repertoire an ability to elicit responses from the spirits to questions posed by participants, thus providing the essential framework of the modern séance. They called themselves "mediums," conduits for dialogue with inhabitants of the Great Beyond. So popular were they that in 1850 they were profitably exhibited by P. T. Barnum at his American Museum in New York.

By then it had become apparent that Spiritualism had struck a real chord in the popular imagination. The quality of mediumship, it turned out, was by no means confined to the Fox sisters. In 1851 it was estimated that there were fifty mediumistic circles in Brooklyn alone, and by 1853 practicing Spiritualists in New York City were said to number some forty thousand. Boston, Columbus, Cleveland, Cincinnati, and Chicago all contained numerous Spiritualist circles. Exclusively Spiritualist communities were briefly established in Mountain Cove, Virginia; Chautaqua County, New York; and Harmony Springs, Arkansas. Throughout the 1850s, others gifted with the Fox sisters' mediumistic abilities, in all regions of the nation and its territories, enlisted the curious into what were usually small, semi-private circles for the purpose of establishing discourse with the dead.[3]

Mediums were often addressed by the spirits via the practice of "slate writing," wherein writing appeared inexplicably on a slate held by the medium, and the message made sense to one or more participants in the séance. In addition, the spirits often announced their presence even more palpably through physical phenomena such as the tilting of tables, the playing of musical instruments, and even full or partial materializations of themselves. The addition of physical manifestations to the range of phenomena recorded by Spiritualists underscores the most singular theme in Spiritualist practice: the emphasis on observable, empirical verifications of the unseen world and its inhabitants.

E. M. Capron, in the introduction to his account of Spiritualism (1855), supplied this remarkably clear expression of the peculiar scientism of the Spiritualist enterprise as Spiritualists themselves saw it:

> I disclaim at the outset all intentions of advocating *super*naturalism. . . .
> The entire separation [between "nature" and "spirit"] made by the old *philosophy* and theology, has led thousands of philosophical minds to reject all ideas of any existence of persons beyond the tangible forms which men now occupy. They have failed entirely of obtaining, from old traditions, proof which looked rational to them of any such existence. . . . Men of philosophical minds, not having positive proof of spiritual existence, have discovered this glaring inconsistency, and rejected any theory offered in favor of existence beyond the decay of the visible body. But the developments of the last few years in clairvoyance and psychology have convinced many of the skeptics in regard to future

existence that there is a positive identity of spirits of persons who have passed beyond this state of existence.[4]

So convinced were many Spiritualists of the scientific validity of what they had witnessed that professional scientists and even a congressional committee were urged to investigate.[5] Spiritualists continued to insist on the empirical authenticity of séance-parlor phenomena, despite sensational disclosures of mediumistic fraud throughout the 1850s and 1860s.[6]

Séances were the central Spiritualist experience (or, perhaps, form of worship). On that foundation, however, an enormously heterogeneous array of specific beliefs and organizational forms was built. Spiritualism as a practice presented itself to society in a variety of ways, from private home circles to public mediumistic demonstrations; from local "centers" or churches to explicitly Spiritualist communities; from published announcements that the spirits confirmed the ministry of Jesus to those reporting that they had reformulated it.[7] But after the 1870s, that lack of centralized organization combined with other factors (for example, the hostility of the press and the established churches) to erode its stature. Spiritualist organizations and publications became much less public a part of the sociocultural fabric of American life. Spiritualist practice, while never disappearing, became much more marginal and private an activity.[8]

But by then the mediums had carried their craft to Britain, where Spiritualism enjoyed a steady if modest development after less spectacular beginnings. As early as 1852, the American medium Mrs. Hayden had visited England to give a number of sittings, at a guinea apiece, for the educated classes. The table-tilting craze that followed, abetted by both American and British mediums, marked the beginning of Spiritualism on the American model in Britain. Physicist Michael Faraday's explanation of the matter suggested that the movement of furniture was caused not by unseen spiritual entities but by the unnoticed muscular activity of séance participants.[9] However, Spiritualism in Britain survived his analysis and succeeded, as in America, in extending itself beyond genteel circles into a wide range of social strata.[10] In Britain, as in America, it was a diffuse phenomenon with no socially differentiated constituency, no standardized body of beliefs, and at best a shifting and fragmented organizational apparatus.[11] Yet, as in America, it survived as a practice well into the twentieth century.

The peculiarly amorphous and disjointed quality of Spiritualism as a movement makes it difficult to analyze as a historical phenomenon, and may in part account for the scant attention it has received from scholars. Most of those few who have addressed it have recognized that Spiritualism must be understood first as a personal experience. That personal experience can be grasped through the enormous body of literature on Spiritualism by nineteenth-century British and American Spiritualists themselves.[12] This literature strongly suggests that for Spiritualists the problem of death was the salient one. To them, human selfhood was noumenal precisely because bodily death did not extinguish it, precisely because it was related to an "other" dimension in a bond that death did not sever. In fact, the personal survival of death was, to Spiritualists, the only conceivable confirmation of noumenal selfhood.

If there is a "typical" personal encounter with Spiritualism, it would proceed along the following lines. A relative or close friend dies, and an acute bereavement is for some reason not sufficiently tempered by traditional religious explanations of death's meaning within the cosmic scheme of things. Yet at the same time, a general philosophical disorientation attendant on the newly deepened appreciation of the reality of death is not assuaged by mere dismissal of the religious interpretation. The problem raises the entire question of the nature of human existence, both its quality and its ultimate purpose.

Eventually, certain occurrences (dreams, unexplained noises, even the page at which a book is casually opened or the lyrics of an overheard tune) suggest that the departed is making an attempt at communication. At this point, a "home circle" of sympathetic confreres may assemble to join hands by candlelight and try somehow to contact the mysterious entity. Hymns will be sung, brows furrowed in intense silent concentration, and, inevitably, a rap will be heard, a curtain will billow, a table will move. The sitting will be found tantalizing but empirically unsatisfying and, purely in the spirit of scientific inquiry, further attempts will be made. Enter the medium.

Visits to the medium, for either private or group séances, will be undertaken over an extended period of time, and are acknowledged to vary in results achieved. But sooner or later phenomena will be witnessed, with the observer's own eyes and ears, that seriously challenge his or her skepticism. Lights will flash. Tables will rock. Gusts of wind of unascertainable origin—even touches—will be felt. In dim light, writing will wondrously appear on slate boards. Most startling of all, peculiar substances may emanate from a cabinet in the medium's séance room (inspected beforehand, of course, and found to be empty). These substances will take the form of hands, limbs, a head, even perhaps an entire human form. If so, the form (often an American Indian or a celebrated historical personage) will introduce itself as the medium's spirit guide or "control." Alternatively, the "control" may not evidence itself through materialization but rather through the medium's own body. In a deep trance and apparently oblivious to all, the medium's voice will change into something not recognizably his or her own and will announce that a new spirit personality now inhabits the corporal form. The sitter, hard-headed and empirical, is not immediately impressed. What has been witnessed up to this point could perhaps be explained as conjuring or sophisticated fakery. But when the spirit control reveals knowledge of both sitter and departed of a deeply private nature—which no one else could *possibly* have known—skepticism finally crumbles.

The experience has been a heady one. It may lead to continued visits, switching mediums as their powers decline. It may lead to attempts to develop a mediumistic aptitude personally. It may lead to participation in a Spiritualist church, perhaps even an evangelical career. The spirits may describe life in the spirit world (almost invariably very similar to life "on the earthly plane"). They may arrange conversations with selected inhabitants of various spiritual "levels."

They may offer personally relevant advice. They may even advance opinions on world affairs. But the one unvarying common element is what has happened to the sitter, to his or her convictions and understanding of reality.

With his or her own eyes and ears the sitter has learned that spirits in fact exist. The soul has been empirically confirmed. In that it survives death, human personality is actually numinous after all.

Spiritualism's appeal could and did reach individuals in any and all social locations.[13] Even moderns often find something creative, perhaps something oddly touching, in its insistence that a rational, scientific epistemology did not deny but actually verified the reality of the soul. However, Spiritualists in the mid- and late nineteenth century ran into serious, stubborn opposition.

To begin with, Spiritualism at the time of its greatest prominence struck a raw nerve in denominational Protestantism. Conservatives simply railed against defections from the established churches, but the liberal clergy found in Spiritualism a deeper dilemma. As they knew, Spiritualism in its own strange way actually mirrored the ideals of nineteenth-century liberal Protestantism. Its attempted rapprochement with scientific thought reflected liberal theology's theme of demystification, while the Spiritualists' intensely personalized conviction of noumenal selfhood reflected liberal insistence on the removal of encumbrances on individual spiritual impulses. But, at the same time, even liberals had to feel alarmed at some Spiritualists' complete dismissal of the Scriptures in favor of mediumistic phenomena as transmitters, as it were, of the Word. While modernist theologians struggled mightily to reconcile revelation and natural law, Spiritualists blithely announced that they had already done so. Many felt no further need for theologians, churches, or even the Bible. What Spiritualism may have represented to the organized religions was an image of where a nonstandardized interpretation of personal ontological status, divorced for all practical purposes from institutional guidance, could lead. Judging from clerical responses, it is difficult to tell what it was about Spiritualism that upset liberal Protestants more: mediumistic chicanery that undermined the entire idea of rational religion or the types of social and political behavior Spiritualists seemed to be learning from their personal conversations with departed souls. [14]

The ways in which American Spiritualists actually *acted* on the reaffirmed conviction of the reality of their own souls were indeed distinctive. There was an extraordinary Spiritualist zeal for social reform on moral grounds (the effectiveness of which was severely undercut by the Spiritualists' extremely individualistic conceptions of appropriate moral action). Convinced that they were in fact individually endowed with a soul, and that the soul carried with it the command to strive for moral perfection, American Spiritualists acted prominently in reform movements from temperance and abolition to free love and utopian socialism. [15] The conviction of noumenal selfhood seems to have promoted personal involvement in a number of enterprises quite disruptive to America's sociopolitical status quo. This also helped wear out Spiritualism's welcome in American society.

But the most deadly opponents of Spiritualism were found where Spiritualists themselves probably least expected genuine vitriol: the scientific world. That brand of opposition was most pronounced, and most consequential, in Britain.

THE REJECTION OF THE SPIRITUALIST RAPPROCHEMENT IN BRITAIN

Science in Victorian Britain was built on inductive epistemological dicta derived primarily from John Stuart Mill. Chief among these was the claim that meaningful truth is observable or phenomenological truth. In this, the Spiritualists concurred. They felt that mediumistic phenomena merited, at the very least, serious consideration from scientists precisely because in those phenomena the soul was manifest to the senses. But they didn't understand that to many Victorian scientists "Science" meant more than the attempted application of empiricist observational techniques to any chosen phenomenon. "Science" was a considerably more grandiose notion, involving not just empiricist

methods but an empiricist assessment of reality. Its proponents held
that True Science meant a portrayal of the world in toto in which
objective or empirically observable data were emphasized as the most
meaningful, the most important and efficacious components in human
understandings of reality.[16] The issue was vastly more complex than
most Spiritualists ever realized. Victorian scientists could hardly mus-
ter enthusiasm for "empirical" demonstrations of the soul, when "the
soul" itself was one of those wholly interior or subjectively sustained
categories of reality (like "aesthetics" or "mind") whose importance,
they felt, should be reduced in man's appreciation of his world. It was
not that Victorian scientists tried, collectively, to eliminate such
categories from human consciousness, or even that they thought objective data necessarily exhaustive of reality. It was rather that, by and
large, they wanted the importance of empirically known or knowable
categories enhanced in the conceptual apparatus with which men cope
with the world. The sense of mission in the scientific community and
the militant scientism of Victorian intellectual life in general has often
been noted by historians.[17] Professional scientists themselves often
believed that a corrective was required for that form of consciousness
(often loosely labeled "metaphysical") that they felt had been dominant
until their own time. That form, they felt, had yielded only a false
appreciation of the world, and an inability to master it materially.
Thomas Huxley was always particularly vociferous in his insistence that
the scientific perspective be adopted as the cultural underpinning of
modern civilization itself.[18]

The conviction that it was actually necessary to reconstruct the
entire conceptual apparatus of man helps account for the willingness of
many Victorian scientists to attack religious interpretations of the universe. Neither Francis Bacon nor the men of the seventeenth-century
scientific revolution, despite their commitment to rational explanations
of nature, had in any way intended a serious assault on traditional
religious sentiments. On the contrary, they felt their work comple-
mented the concept of God the Lawgiver by explicating the ordered
operations of his creations. Victorian scientists, on the other hand, were

quite willing to use scientific findings as weapons for discrediting religious formulations. The main target, of course, was the Book of Genesis; and the main weapon was the theory of natural selection. It was not coincidental that Darwin's strongest supporter, Thomas Huxley, was also among the most active champions of "Scientific Naturalism" in general. In addition to the theory of natural selection, weapons in the antireligious arsenal were provided by what we now call "the mechanistic world view," to which so many Victorian scientists committed themselves. That term refers primarily to an embellishment of Newtonian physics attributed to Maxwell (electromagnetic radiation), Kelvin (heat), and especially Dalton (the atomic theory of matter). On the basis of those advances, many scientists claimed that man's total physical and natural environment was explainable with recourse to neither Genesis nor any other religious account.

There was, in fact, a highly vocal cadre of scientific publicists who actively proselytized for the scientific view of life and the world as one in which religious cosmologies and "metaphysical" considerations simply played no part. In addition to Huxley, that cadre of publicists included physicist John Tyndall, mathematician W. K. Clifford, eugenicist and statistician Sir Francis Galton, historian and psychologist G. H. Lewes, biologist E. Ray-Lankester, philosopher Herbert Spencer, essayist Leslie Stephen, and many others. If they sometimes seemed strident in their opposition to religion, it was because in their view religious personnel (especially Anglicans) were often overtly antagonistic and deliberately obstructionist toward science. Bishop Wilberforce's denunciation of Darwinian theory was the most obvious embodiment of opposition to scientific advance. But to many Victorian scientists, he was only the most visible member of an antiscientific element in Britain that ought to be rooted out. The role of religion in educational institutions particularly alarmed the scientific publicists. Some argued that clerical personnel should be replaced by scientists in all phases of the educational process.[19] These were the voices Beatrice Webb heard preaching a "religion of science," the ones expressing "an implicit faith that by the methods of physical science, and by those methods alone, could be solved all the problems arising out of the relations of man to man and of man towards the universe."[20] In such a climate, it is scarcely surprising that Spiritualists could find little welcome in scientific circles. Few scientists even deigned to look into Spiritualist phenomena at all. The matter went deeper than what was, quite often, the hopeless naiveté of the Spiritualists' own standards of evidence. It involved what Spiritualists, in their insistence on the reality of the soul, stood for.

That, at any rate, was how one Spiritualist saw it, and he was in a position to know. Alfred Russel Wallace, codiscoverer with Darwin of biological evolution through natural selection, had been showered with honors. Yet he kept himself aloof from the scientific community and publicly criticized the "materialist" values of Victorian scientists. Wallace had always been deeply concerned with questions of morality, which he felt began with the affirmation of human worth. He believed scientific knowledge was useless unless it contributed to the moral betterment of the species by somehow deepening that affirmation. On that basis, rather than stress biological determinism, Wallace recast his own version of evolution to emphasize mankind's capacity to transcend material circumstances. To Wallace, Victorian scientists' failure to consider the implications their work held for moral behavior indicated severely misplaced priorities. In Spiritualism's demonstration of the reality of the soul, he himself found a basis for belief in moral as well as material evolution. Scientists' refusal to address so important a matter, Wallace believed, revealed an amoral materialism and, as such, outright dereliction of scientific duty.[21]

Wallace was a member of a debating club called the London Dialectical Society, composed mostly of barristers, physicians, and other professional men. Early in 1869, the club decided to make a serious inquiry into Spiritualist phenomena. A special investigative committee was formed, which issued invitations to professional scientists to join in. Those invitations were almost unanimously rejected. T. H. Huxley replied: "Supposing the phenomena to be genuine, they do not interest me. If anybody would endow one with the faculty of listening to the chatter of old women and curates in the nearest cathedral town, I should decline the privilege, having better things to do. And if the folk in the spirit world do not talk more wisely than their friends report them to do, I put them in the same category."[22] But, undeterred, the committee went ahead with its work. Eventually, it published a report declaring that "the subject is worthy of more serious attention than it has received."[23]

The attention Spiritualism would receive, however, was undoubtedly not what A. R. Wallace or any of its supporters had had in mind.

The chemist William Crookes was one of the few Victorian scientists of any note who shared Wallace's interest in Spiritualist phenomena. Crookes' professional credentials were impressive: discoverer of the metallic chemical element thallium, fellow of the Royal Society, coeditor of the *Quarterly Journal of Science*. In the July 1870 edition of that journal, he had announced his intention of applying rigorously professional experimental controls to mediumistic manifestations. Spiritualists, he said, spoke of bodies weighing fifty pounds and more being levitated and whole houses being shaken by the spirits. He would merely require them, under proper test conditions, to start a pendulum swinging. Crookes chose as his subject not just any medium but the remarkable Daniel Dunglas Home. That selection was not arbitrary.

Home was by far the most famous medium practicing in Britain at the time. He was capable of producing table motion, automatic writing, spirit materialization, and even the levitation of his own person. His manifestations outstripped anything British Spiritualists had yet seen, and he was never detected, with anything approaching conclusive proof, in fraud. His reputation was international. In Paris, he levitated a table with Prince Murat holding its feet while Napoleon III watched, and materialized a ghostly hand to write "Napoleon" in the earlier Bonaparte's script. Home was conspicuous among mediums in that he never charged for his services (he did, however, accept voluntary contributions). By opting to test this particular figure, Crookes made sure his study would be an important one for the image of Spiritualism among the general public.[24]

Their encounter was indeed startling. The chemist had created mechanical devices for his experiments, with which he said Home was unacquainted and thus unable to manipulate. In one experiment, an accordion was placed in a wire cage with its keys on the bottom, and Home was allowed to touch it with only one hand. The accordion began to expand, contract, and play music. It even briefly floated. In another experiment, a scale's pointer oscillated as Home approached it, although he had exerted no pressure on the object it weighed. Crookes actually claimed, on the basis of these and other experiments, that he had established "the existence of a new force, in some unknown manner connected with the human organization."[25]

The publication of Crookes' paper happened to coincide with a particularly bizarre Spiritualist incident (the alleged disappearance and relocation of the medium Mrs. Guppy) that had received considerable attention in the press. To scientists, Crookes' work with Home may have appeared likely to encourage what already seemed a dangerously extensive public tolerance or even endorsement of Spiritualism. At any rate, the scientific community responded to Crookes' work in a manner that could leave little doubt as to the attitude most scientists held toward Spiritualism in general, and any association of professional scientists with it in particular.

The attack began with an article entitled "Spiritualism and its Recent Converts" in the *Quarterly Review* of October 1871. The anonymous author dealt with the Guppy incident by casually referring to the transmigrating medium's considerable bulk, and then went on to the more serious business of the Crookes experiments. The article submitted that Crookes had not adequately controlled against Home's ability to distract the experimenter's attention and apply his own gadgets to the equipment. It concluded by very strongly inferring that Crookes the scientist was not worthy of the name. Referring to

Crookes' membership in the Royal Society, the author actually bordered on slander by averring that:

> this distinction was conferred on him with considerable hesitation, the ability he displayed in the investigation of thallium being purely *technical*. We are advised, on the highest authority, that he is regarded among chemists as a specialist of specialists, being totally destitute of any knowledge of Chemical Philosophy, and utterly untrustworthy as to any inquiry which requires more than technical knowledge for its successful conduct.

Although the article was unsigned, its author was known to be W. B. Carpenter.[26] Carpenter was a fellow of the Royal Society and registrar at London University. He was also the author of the leading physiological textbooks, and had argued for some time that forms of "unconscious cerebration," translated into the muscular activity to which Faraday had attributed table-turning, were at the root of whatever Spiritualist phenomena remained after fraud was eliminated. He was to become one of the most vocal critics of Spiritualism, and particularly of scientists connected with it. The personal attack he mounted against Crookes indicated that he was willing to go to rather extreme lengths in discouraging scientists' involvement in Spiritualism, and whatever aura of scientific legitimacy might accrue to it as a result.

Crookes, stung, took steps to learn how representative of his professional colleagues' views Carpenter's attack really was. He presented a paper on the Home experiments to the Council of the Royal Society. It was returned with a request for additional evidence. He presented a second paper, and it was rejected outright. Next, the chemist lodged a formal complaint with the Royal Society against the author of "Spiritualism and its Recent Converts." Crookes charged that the author had referred without authorization to council discussions in an attempt to slander him. He requested a formal rebuke. The council replied with a mild resolution regretting that statements in the article had indeed referred without authorization to council deliberations. But it specifically refused to rebuke the author. On the contrary, the Association for the Advancement of Science showed its support for Carpenter's position by electing him president for the following year.[27]

Crookes responded to this obvious, semiofficial censure of his own position by immersing himself even further in Spiritualism.[28] His continuing publications on the subject in the *Quarterly Journal of Science* even helped prompt a handful of other scientists (Lord Rayleigh, Balfour Stewart) to undertake their own independent investigations. But the leaders of the Royal Society and the Association for the Advancement of Science had clearly demonstrated the position of mainstream scientific thought on the subject of Spiritualism. And that was just the beginning.

Professor E. Ray-Lankester was a young biologist who, along with Carpenter, had taken up the cause of anti-Spiritualist activism. In 1876, Ray-Lankester claimed to have attended a séance at which he had openly detected the medium Henry Slade in fraud. Slade specialized in slate writing and was well known as a personal favorite of Wallace. But Ray-Lankester stated that he had snatched a slate away from Slade with a spirit's message written on it before the spirit in question had even begun its communication. The biologist actually filed legal suit against Slade. Under the Vagrancy Acts, he charged the medium with "unlawfully using subtle craft, means, and devices to deceive and impose upon certain of Her Majesty's subjects." He was accompanied in the suit by the physician Horatio Donkin, another anti-Spiritualist crusader.[29]

The cause became a *cause célèbre* for Spiritualists because it was an act not of passive disdain but of active hostility by representatives of the scientific community. *The Times* reported on October 11 that the court was thronged and the street outside barely passable because of the interest the case had generated among Spiritualists. Ray-Lankester, acknowledging that he himself could not qualify as a skilled observer, had testimony introduced from the professional conjurer John Maskelyne to the effect that Slade was a common, in fact rather maladroit, trickster. Maskelyne claimed that Slade's "slate writing" technique consisted of holding a slate under a table with his hands, which thus seemed occupied and unable to produce the writing that subsequently appeared on the slate. He pointed to bars and wedges under the table, which he said held the slate and freed the medium's hands to write on it. With the table as an exhibit, Ray-Lankester and Donkin filed suit against Slade's assistant as well because the assistant had specified the details of the table's construction. Then, with two men involved, the plaintiffs could add the charge of conspiracy, in case the vagrancy charge should fail. Obviously Ray-Lankester and Donkin wanted results. They wanted what they felt to be mediumistic chicanery not just exposed but punished, and Spiritualism itself discouraged.

Wallace himself was subpoenaed to give evidence for the defense. He testified that on prior occasions he had seen Slade produce effects that in his opinion could not have involved sleight of hand. In addition, the carpenters who built the table said its bars and wedges had been added not on specification but to compensate for faulty workmanship. But nothing could save Slade. The judge found him guilty of willfully deceiving Ray-Lankester for profit, and gave him the maximum punishment allowed under the law: three months' hard labor. The case was later overturned on a technicality, but Slade fled the country anyway.

The effects of the Slade case can easily be imagined. In the Crookes affair, the Royal Society and the Association for the Advancement of Science had not just countered a Spiritualist interpretation of certain phenomena but had tacitly endorsed a condemnation of the investigator. The Slade case supplemented that expression of anti-Spiritualist sentiment within the scientific community by serving notice that prominent mediums actually risked prosecution if their evidence of contact with the spirits was not very convincing indeed.

Spiritualism was not about to collapse as a mass practice. Nor were Wallace, Crookes, or any of the other intellectual figures with an interest in it dissuaded from their inquiries and, occasionally, their evangelism. But it had been made clear that mainstream scientific thought was unreceptive, to say the least, toward what Spiritualists had

actually thought was a rapprochement between science and religion.
From the Spiritualist point of view, the question was: what next?

NOTES

1. Unfortunately, the public record of Spiritualism must be gleaned, piecemeal, from a variety of sources. The best contemporary accounts of Spiritualist phenomena and practices, and their spread throughout the United States and Britain, are probably: E. W. Capron, *Modern Spiritualism: Its Facts and Fanaticisms, Its Consistencies and Contradictions* (Boston: Bela Marsh, 1855); Frank Podmore, *Modern Spiritualism,* vols. 1 and 2 (London: Methuen, 1902); and Emma Hardinge-Britten, *Modern American Spiritualism* (New York: The National Spiritualist Association, 1870). The only major examples of professional historical or sociological scholarship on the subject to date are: G. K. Nelson, *Spiritualism and Society* (New York: Schocken, 1969); Burton Gates Brown, "Spiritualism in Nineteenth Century America" (Ph.D. dissertation in history, Boston University, 1973); and R. Laurence Moore's excellent *In Search of White Crows: Spiritualism, Parapsychology, and American Culture* (New York: Oxford University Press, 1977).

2. Nelson, *Spiritualism and Society,* pp. 52–54.

3. Ibid., pp. 8–20.

4. Capron, *Modern Spiritualism,* pp. 12–13.

5. The only important scientific investigation actually undertaken in the United States, however, was that of the University of Pennsylvania's Seybert Commission. It published only one report, which dwelled largely on dishonest mediums (*Preliminary Report of the Commission Appointed by the University of Pennsylvania to Investigate Modern Spiritualism* [Philadelphia: J. B. Lippincott, 1887]).

6. G. K. Nelson notes that since mediums were viewed as gifted but replaceable agents for higher powers Spiritualism could actually withstand almost any number of exposures of fraudulent mediums or deterioration of specific mediums' abilities ("The medium may lose his prestige, but the spirits do not lose theirs" [*Spiritualism and Society,* p. 244]).

The most serious disclosure of mediumistic fraud actually occurred in 1888, when Margaret Fox herself confessed that she and her sister had been cracking their toejoints all along. That confession was itself later recanted, and the genuineness of the Fox sisters' mediumship remains a controversial subject among the small but steadfast Spiritualist populations of America and Britain.

7. Burton Gates Brown notes that there was no Spiritualist theology, but rather thousands of separate theologies. With no really coherent creed of its own, Spiritualism could not effectively compete with organized churches and systematic theological schemes (*Spiritualism,* pp. 338–39).

8. Both Burton Gates Brown and R. Laurence Moore agree that the multiplicity of Spiritualist associations and interpretations of the spirits' counsel expressed a radically individualistic, anti-institutional ethic among Spiritualists, and effectively hampered the development of Spiritualism into anything resembling a social "force" or religious "system" (Moore, *In Search of White Crows,* pp. 40–101). Moore notes that many American Spiritualists "tended to treat the divinity of Christ as little more than evidence for the divine side of all men" (p. 55). The organized churches were, not surprisingly, ill-disposed toward theological speculations of that sort. Clerics in both America and Britain tended toward the view that if there were any truth at all in the Spiritualists' claims, then they were in all probability communicating with tarnished and malevolent spirits (see, for example, N. S. Godfrey, *Table-Tilting Tested and Proved to be the Result of Satanic Agency.* London: 1853; or E. Gillson, *Table-Talking: Disclosures of Satanic Wonders.* Bath, England: 1853).

9. *The Times,* June 30, 1853; *Atheneum,* July 2, 1853.

10. While the actual socioeconomic composition of British Spiritualists as a group is difficult to gauge with any precision, it is clear that the movement encompassed, among others, artisans and skilled workers in Yorkshire and Lancashire industrial towns. One of its most active promoters in England, James Burns, organized the Association of Progressive Spiritualists of Great Britain specifically to represent Spiritualism's working-class constituency (Nelson, *Spiritualism and Society,* pp. 100–102).

11. National or centralized Spiritualist organizations were occasionally formed in Britain (the National Association of Spiritualists, the Central Association of Spiritualists, the London Spiritualist Alliance, and so on). But they never managed to bring uniformity or even clarity to Spiritualist beliefs, practices, or intentions. Even the most long-lived group, the National Union of Spiritualists, could never claim representation of all local societies and independent circles (ibid., pp. 89–153).

12. See, for example: Emma Hardinge-Britten, *Nineteenth Century Miracles* (New York, 1884); Catherine Crowe, *The Night Side of Nature* (London, 1852); John Worth Edmonds, *Spiritual Tracts* (New York, 1858); J. S.Rymes, *Spirit Manifestations* (Boston, 1881); and G. W. Stone, *An Exposition of Spirit Manifestations* (London, 1852).

13. Sociologist G. K. Nelson has argued that Spiritualism was (and still is) a response to "social anomie," a socially pervasive normlessness engendered

by extremely rapid and disruptive social change. He notes that modern Spiritualism first emerged in an area (the remarkable "burnt-over district" of western New York State) characterized by widespread social mobility, both vertical and horizontal; a great influx of immigrants bearing divergent cultural traditions; and intensive, compressed industrialization processes. All this, Nelson claims, challenged traditional interpretations of life and the world, and of the individual's proper role in society. Spiritualism to him has constituted an attempt to reconstruct a coherent and tenable value system for individuals by invoking the transcendent authority of the spirits to legitimate it (*Spiritualism and Society*, pp. 217–38).

But that analysis, while it may help clarify Spiritualism's original appearance, does not account for its spread to areas where those social circumstances that characterized the "burnt-over district" are not known to have been at work. In addition, it fails to come to terms with what was really singular about Spiritualism: its claim to "scientific" validity, its assertion of the "empirical" authenticity of the soul. R. Laurence Moore's *In Search of White Crows*, by fitting the phenomenon of Spiritualism into a cultural rather than a structural context, offers a less ambitious but more satisfying analysis of at least the American version.

14. Moore, *In Search of White Crows*, pp. 40–70.

15. Ibid., pp. 70–102.

16. For an excellent discussion of Victorian science and scientists, see Frank Miller Turner's *Between Science and Religion* (New Haven: Yale University Press, 1974), pp. 8–31. Turner terms the output of Victorian scientists "Scientific Naturalism," reflecting their own conviction that they were supplying not merely delimited analyses of discrete aspects of the universe but a new conceptualization of what was truthful and meaningful in the universe.

17. See, for example Walter Houghton, *The Victorian Frame of Mind, 1830–1870* (New Haven: Yale University Press, 1957); H. Grisewood, ed., *Ideas and Beliefs of the Victorians* (New York: E. P. Dutton, 1966); or Richard D. Altick, *Victorian People and Ideas* (New York: World, 1964).

18. See Huxley's *Collected Essays* (New York: Appleton, 1894).

19. See, for instance, John Tyndall's *Fragments of Science*, 6th ed. (New York: Appleton, 1892), pp. 40–45; John Morley's *The Struggle for National Education* (London: Chapman and Hall, 1873); and an anonymous article, "The National Importance of Research," in *Westminster Review*, vol. 99 (1873), pp. 343–66.

20. Beatrice Webb, *My Apprenticeship* (London: Longmans, Green, 1926), p. 83.

21. For material on Wallace see Loren Eiseley's "Alfred Russel Wallace," in *Scientific American*, February 1959; Wilma George's *Biologist*

Philosopher: A Study in the Life and Writings of Alfred Russel Wallace (New York: Abelard-Schuman, 1964); and, especially, Frank Miller Turner's "Wonderful Man of the Wonderful Century" in *Between Science and Religion.* Turner's treatment is the only one that effectively relates Wallace's Spiritualism to his understanding of the purpose of scientific knowledge. Turner also notes the fact that, unlike most Victorian scientists, Wallace had been born poor and was largely self-educated. The distance between Wallace and most other scientists was social as well as intellectual, and his endorsement of Spiritualism may have expressed both aspects.

22. *Report on Spiritualism of the Committee of the London Dialectical Society* (London: Longmans, Green, Read, and Dyer, 1871), pp. 229–30.

23. Ibid., p. 6. The committee had divided into two sections. One collected oral and written testimony on Spiritualism, the other investigated mediums first-hand. That second section in turn had broken down into six smaller groups, and only three of those claimed to have found anything worth reporting. Since the committee's members were actually rather severely divided as to whether or not Spiritualism merited further inquiry, it seems likely that Wallace himself was highly influential in framing the report's final summation. See Alan Gauld's *The Founders of Psychical Research.* (New York: Schocken, 1968), pp. 83–86.

24. Biographical material on this fascinating character comes primarily from his own *Incidents in My Life* (London, 1863) and *Lights and Shadows of Spiritualism* (London, 1877) and from his wife's *The Gift of D. D. Home* (London, 1890). He is the subject of Robert Browning's sarcastic poem, "Mr. Sludge the Medium."

25. *Quarterly Journal of Science,* July 1871.

26. Alan Gauld, *The Founders of Psychical Research,* p. 87.

27. For Crookes' own account of the affair, see his *Researches in the Phenomena of Spiritualism* (London, 1874). It is also treated in Brian Inglis' *Natural and Supernatural: A History of the Paranormal* (London: Hodder and Stoughton, 1977), pp. 253–64.

28. It has been alleged that Crookes' further experiments covered an illicit affair with the medium Florence Cook. See Trevor Hall's *The Spiritualists* (London: Duckworth, 1962).

29. The best account of the Slade trial is in Inglis' *Natural and Supernatural,* pp. 278–81.

Chapter Three

The Formation of the
Society for Psychical Research

GENESIS

Throughout the 1870s, E. Dawson Rogers, vice president of the Central Association of Spiritualists and occasional editor of its periodical, *Light,* found the indifference and hostility of the scientific community matters of serious concern. Rogers felt that if more investigations like that of Crookes on Home could only be undertaken, the authenticity of Spiritualist phenomena might yet be conclusively established. He expected that once Spiritualism was intellectually legitimated in that manner it would grow more rapidly.

It happened that Rogers' interest in furthering professional scientific research into Spiritualist phenomena meshed with the concerns of William Barrett, a professor of Physics at the Royal College of Science in Dublin. Barrett's interest in Spiritualist phenomena, not surprisingly, revolved around the possibilities they presented of some yet unrecognized physical force. His curiosity had been piqued by a set of odd experiences he had had in Ireland. Through a friend who was experimenting with mesmerism, Barrett had found that under trance conditions certain people were capable of a range of perception that he thought so heightened as to indicate some extrasensory vehicle for the conveyance of information. Carpenter himself had accepted the reality of heightened sensory perception in a trance state, but Barrett felt that did not account for all he had witnessed.

In 1876 Barrett had written a paper on the subject for the Association for the Advancement of Science, but it was never published. In fact, it was read only in the anthropological subsection, and there only because of the influence of the chairman, A. R. Wallace.[1] Undeterred by the rebuff, Barrett found a rich experimental situation in the home of the Rev. A. M. Creery of Buxton. Creery's daughters and a maid-servant were able to guess with surprising consistency whatever subject other family members and friends were concentrating on. Barrett reported his findings in an issue of *Nature* in 1881, and determined to press on in this area. Spiritualists, he learned, could refer him to a host of individuals with gifts similar to those on display in the Creery household.

In Barrett, Dawson Rogers found an enthusiastic supporter of the plan to form a new organization dedicated to the scientific investigation of Spiritualist phenomena. Rogers' notion was that while already committed Spiritualists went about their business in their own organizations, a new research society might be formed to break down that image of seedy charlatanism that kept "persons of culture and good social position" away from the movement.[2] From this impetus the Society for Psychical Research was born in 1882.

The first matter on the agenda was who would lead the organization. Barrett and Rogers both wanted someone who was intellectually "respectable," especially to the scientifically minded. Rogers in particular wanted someone with some skill in public relations, as the establishment of a more favorable public image for Spiritualism was his real goal. The man they eventually settled on was Henry Sidgwick, Professor of Moral Philosophy at Cambridge. That choice would decisively influence the entire direction taken in the struggle to preserve the concept of the soul within a rationalistic system of thought. For although Henry Sidgwick was deeply concerned with the idea of the soul, neither Rogers nor Barrett realized, at first, that there were key differences between his intellectual temperament and their own.

During the 1860s, Sidgwick had been among those whose religious ideas were profoundly affected by the Victorian intellectual climate that discouraged or deemphasized nonempirical or "metaphysical" considerations in interpretations of life and the world. His own belief in a linkage between the life of man on earth and a nontemporal realm was severely shaken by Renan and the criticisms of Biblical texts that were current at the time. They and, to a lesser extent, Darwin weakened his conviction that either the life of Jesus or human existence itself was necessarily related to any supernatural dimension of reality or to any cosmic design at all. Unlike some religious intellectuals, Sidgwick was not willing to merely stand in stubborn opposition to the entire intellectual temper of the age. Instead he began looking seriously at Christianity as a historical religion, using Hebrew and Arabic sources. He wanted to determine the degree to which Christianity represented some introjection of a transcendent Creator's intentions into the world and, by implication, the reality of that transcendent realm itself.

His interest was principally in the evidence for miracles in Christianity. But his studies convinced him that the evidence for Christian miracles was no better than that for any other religion's, then finally that the historical evidence for all miracles was categorically unsatisfying. When he found himself unable to accept the Virgin Birth, he severed personal ties to Christianity.[3] Like many Anglicans, Sidgwick was posing the question: when one begins denying miracles, where does one stop?

Sidgwick's religious deconversion expressed his personal adherence to rational empiricism as the means by which the world should be perceived. He took that commitment seriously enough to resign, in 1869, a Trinity fellowship that involved affirmation of the Apostles' Creed. He was promptly appointed to a lectureship in moral sciences at Trinity nonetheless, and it was in that position that his own intellectual dilemma really surfaced. For there was more to Sidgwick's overall intellectual make-up than rational empiricism. He was just as strongly committed to the maintenance of some force for the moral ordering of action in the world. The title "Moral Scientist" was, for Sidgwick, an appropriate one. He saw his job as the construction of a system of human ethics that satisfied rationalist criteria of intellectual validity. It is risky to simplify Sidgwick's enormously complex and richly textured thought. Nevertheless, it might be said that while he found Christianity incompatible with scientific reason, he was hard-pressed to conceptualize "morality" without the logical legitimations which grand religious formulations such as Christianity had previously supplied.

Sidgwick's problem was a stark one. He required, as his first principle, a definition of "good." Arguing from a fundamentally utilitarian perspective, he considered the only possible definition of good to be personal happiness. But Sidgwick believed very firmly that personal happiness and social responsibility were never entirely compatible. While the specific strictures of Christianity had to be dismissed, something had to be found that could effectively duplicate their tempering effect on selfishness. To Sidgwick, Christianity had been an unscientific fraud. But without it, he feared his own society would lack any intellectually defensible encouragement of limitations on personal pleasure. Without a solution in the form of a system of ethics on a firmly rationalistic foundation, Sidgwick could foresee little but social chaos and an uninhabitable world.[4]

For his ethical system to achieve coherence, Sidgwick found himself required to postulate that the human personality survives bodily death, so that the sacrifice of personal gratification necessitated by social duty could eventually be compensated. Demonstration of that survival became, for Sidgwick, something of an obsession. During the 1870s, he led a group of Cambridge intellectuals into an informal investigation of Spiritualist phenomena. Henry Slade had been one of their subjects. Their sittings with him had occurred prior to the medium's public disgrace, but even then Sidgwick had not been particularly impressed. In fact, the Sidgwick group's inquiry into Spiritualism, while intriguing, had not been particularly successful. What was sought had not been found.

To Barrett and Rogers, Sidgwick's skepticism regarding Spiritualism actually seemed something of a virtue. Given his reputation, no one could believe that any organization under his direction would include anyone, or undertake anything, naive or dishonest.[5] Especially from Rogers' point of view, Sidgwick had additional qualifications to lead the new Society for Psychical Research. At Cambridge, he had worked on behalf of women's education and had demonstrated a real skill in the establishment of a positive public image for that cause. Also, Sidgwick's marriage to Eleanor Balfour (whose brother Arthur, the future prime minister, had been one of his students) provided an entree into the highest social circles. But Rogers didn't understand Sidgwick's own assessment of Spiritualism and the proper means to demonstrate the existence of the soul in a rationalist culture.

Sidgwick knew that to scientists Spiritualism was an attempt to affirm something that could not be seriously entertained within an authentically scientific appreciation of the world: some normally unseen dimension of existence, the "spirit," the soul. Spiritualists claimed that the spirit manifested itself empirically. But the problem for scientists was that "spirit" itself was not a meaningful category of reality. Spiritualism's entire thrust was toward verification of some immortal component of human selfhood. But the entire orientation of science was toward the here and now, toward precisely what *is* mortal, what *is* temporal, what *is* contained within our own space-time continuum. In short, Victorian science as Sidgwick saw it was an explicitly secular (in fact, often an intentionally secularizing) enterprise in that it encouraged a cognitive orientation toward *this* world. Sidgwick knew that making the notion that some part of ourselves survives death at all meaningful would require a more substantial accommodation to the scientific perspective than Spiritualists had ever really made. It would be necessary to reveal that part of ourselves that was operating in the here and now. It would be necessary to locate the spirit as a phenomenon of this world, not merely point to its extraordinary intrusions into this world from another.

That would mean a search for a component of human personality that somehow functioned outside or beyond the constraints of the perishable body. Sidgwick felt he might find what he sought somewhere among those phenomena that indicated human mental activity was occurring outside recognized physiological channels. Somehow he hoped to demonstrate the existence of nonmaterial mind: the stuff (or, paradoxically, "nonstuff") of which "spirit" might be made. In Barrett's findings on thought-reading, he saw the possibility of taking the next step toward elaborating a version of "spirit" that would be compatible with the scientific point of view, and with rationalized culture generally. In the Society for Psychical Research, he saw the opportunity to actually secularize the soul.[6]

Organization and Personnel of the S.P.R.

In the spring and early summer of 1882, a series of meetings was held by the Society's founders to plan its future.[7] A major consideration at that stage was the recruitment of members. Not surprisingly, the Society's early membership was drawn primarily from Spiritualist ranks, especially from the Central Association of Spiritualists. But one prominent member of the C.A.S., the medium William Stainton Moses, was chary of the whole enterprise, and had to be convinced by Rogers to lend his support.[8] A major editorial contributor to *Light* and a medium of conspicuously unblemished personal reputation, Moses had been investigated by members of the Sidgwick circle, with inconclusive results. His reluctance to involve himself in the new field of psychical research seems to have stemmed from certain misgivings about the direction it might take under Sidgwick's leadership. The earliest indication of that direction could have been found in the constitutional structure of the S.P.R. itself.

The Society's president was to retire yearly and be eligible for reelection up to three years consecutively. He was to supply formal, executive leadership through his *ex officio* participation in all S.P.R. investigative endeavors. The choice of the president was left to a governing council of approximately twenty individuals, one third of whom were elected yearly by the general membership. The council was to have a variety of official responsibilities.[9] Its essential function, however, was monitoring the actual work of the S.P.R. and presenting that work to British society at large. The investigating committees of the

Society would be where "psychical research" would really define itself. The council would oversee their activities and determine which portions were to be disseminated. That is, the actual substance of psychical research was to begin in the investigating committees, then be processed and finally represented to the public by the council.[10]

Getting a certain kind of material before the public was, of course, the whole purpose of the Society from the point of view of Rogers and the other Spiritualists involved in its formation. But even in the beginning they might have wondered a bit about the sort of material the Society was being structured to turn out. It could be seen in the research areas for which investigative committees were formally instituted that the scope of psychical research would not really correspond to that of Spiritualism proper, at least not as Spiritualism had been understood until then. The first of these committees was on thought reading or "thought transference," the area into which Barrett had originally ventured. With Barrett's work as a base, that committee's branch of research was explicitly intended to serve as the cornerstone of future work. Thought transference, in fact, was officially designated "the branch of our research in which hitherto the most progress has been made," its priority as a research zone deemed "right and natural" for "till this comparatively simple class of facts shall have been widely and intelligently recognised, our efforts in other directions must fail of their full effect."[11]

A second committee was to inquire into the question of mesmerism. The Society's leaders felt mesmerism might be related to thought transference, or might reveal another aspect of the same mental quality. ("Many, at least, of the commonly reported mesmeric phenomena consist partly of some transmission of thought or sensation from the operator to the subject.")[12] The mesmeric committee was "especially anxious to witness cases of what it termed *mesmeric lucidity* or *clairvoyance*," which was distinguished from thought transference in that the former was an entirely individual, not interactional, phenomenon. In a similar vein, a "Reichenbach" committee was instituted to deal with evidence of the "odic force."[13] Another committee was formed for haunted houses. Another was to look into "the physical phenomena of the so-called Spiritualism." Finally, a literary committee was to collect both historical material and contemporary testimony related to any of the other research areas.

With "the so-called Spiritualism" forming only one subject of the S.P.R.'s investigations, it was clear that the focus of psychical research was to be on the mind, specifically on phenomena that indicated mental activity occurring independently of the senses or of physical matter altogether. The implications that the establishment of "non-material mind" might eventually hold for Spiritualism were obvious. But drawing the connection between the two would be the responsibility of the committees and the council members themselves. If Stainton Moses or any of the other Spiritualists were watching, a further indication of the direction in which psychical research was headed could have been found in the actual personnel staffing the S.P.R.'s organizational sinews.

When Sidgwick accepted the presidency of the S.P.R., he brought into it a group of friends and Cambridge associates who shared his general intellectual orientations toward "mind" and toward Spiritualism. These included his wife Eleanor Mildred Sidgwick; Richard Hodgson; Frank Podmore; Edmund Gurney; Frederic W. H. Myers; and Myers' brother, the physician Arthur. This little circle, "the Cambridge group," was distinguished from the larger, overtly Spiritualist element in the Society in important respects. First, they held the president's trust. Second, and perhaps more significantly, they had either enough money or the sheer resolve to afford sizable investments of time and energy in psychical research as the S.P.R. had framed it. They were the ones most able and willing to undertake long-term research projects on the various committees. They were the ones most able and willing to assume council responsibilities and participate regularly in its deliberations. They did not comprise a majority among the S.P.R.'s active workers, but they were a powerful little clique that, under Sidgwick's guidance, could effectively determine the actual contours of psychical research. [14]

In a sense, psychical research was to be hewn from Spiritualism by the committees and by the council, under Sidgwick's direction. Members of the Cambridge group would sculpt its form, and two of them, especially, would throw themselves into the field wholeheartedly. Those two, F. W. H. Myers and Edmund Gurney, had a rather distinctive perspective on spiritual matters. They were actually interested in tapping, experiencing and feeling what was spiritual within themselves.

Myers' lineage was old Yorkshire gentry. His father had been a well-to-do clergyman and philanthropist in Keswick, Cumberland, when Frederic was born in 1843. Myers was later to recall the parsonage where he was raised in idyllic terms, noting that "the memories of those years swim and sparkle in a haze of light and dew" and that "the thought of Paradise is interwoven for me with that Garden's glory."[15] But even at an early age, the beguilement of pleasant surroundings was undercut by a numbing, inextinguishable sense of dread. Myers' great fear, from childhood throughout the rest of his life, was not pain or failure or loneliness or any of the mundane terrors that haunt most people. It was, rather, a deep horror of the extinction of personality. Around the age of five or six, he experienced his first exposure to the idea of nothingness upon observing a mole crushed under the wheel of a cart. He asked his mother if it would go to heaven, and was aghast to learn that it had no soul and was utterly, undeniably, and inalterably dead. "The pity of it!" he later recalled thinking. "And the first horror of a death without resurrection rose in my bursting heart."[16] Later, when he was about seven, his mother casually suggested that perhaps men who led bad lives on earth were annihilated at death. Little Frederic was again staggered by the very notion. "I remember where I stood at the moment, and how my brain reeled under the shock."[17]

Fear of death is not at all uncommon, but Myers' overwhelming terror of it was special. It seems best understood as the logical correlate of his equally overwhelming love of a certain kind of life, what he called "the inner life." F. W. H. Myers was one of those odd, vaguely disconcerting men whose energies are spent trying to achieve, sustain, and perfect purely subjective forms of experience. His entire history is one long record of attempts to find some almost mystical level of sentience, entirely within himself. For someone as fundamentally self-absorbed as Myers, the extinction of personality might indeed be an uncommonly horrifying prospect.

Myers' father died in 1851. In 1856 his mother took Frederic and her two younger sons to Cheltenham so the children could attend Cheltenham College. Frederic went on to a classical, then a mathematical tutor. At age seventeen ("far too early") he entered Trinity College, Cambridge. While at Cambridge, Myers' "inner life" was dominated by what he called "Hellenism." He had, in adolescence, begun translating Greek and Latin poets, and his increasing immersion in these works provided a rapturous range of experiences he described as "intensifications of my own being," a sense of barely describable exaltation, wonder, and beauty. He "worshipped" Virgil, found "intoxicating joy" in Sappho, entered "another epoch" with Pindar.[18]

Yet the Hellenism of his Cambridge days did not provide the type of subjective vision to which Myers aspired. In fact, in later years he considered it downright base. What is remarkable about Myers is that by "the inner life" he did not mean mere sensuality or egoism. Actually, in his estimation they were the inner life's least desirable, most "common" components. In his autobiography he discusses, shamefacedly, an incident at Cambridge that revealed to him the shortcomings of the extreme glorification of emotion, sensation, and self he found in the classics. Having won a Latin poem prize, he became intoxicated by his own grandeur ("I was fond of alluding to myself as a kind of Virgil among my young companions"). Preparing to write another, he inserted into his own effort selections from a set of Oxford prizewinners "in order to gloat over their inferiority to my own."[19] Myers joked that he was "collecting gold from Ennius' dung-heap," but when his work again won the prize a competitor discovered the insertions and lodged a complaint. The master of Trinity, although aware that nothing actually illegal had been done, advised the preening author to resign his prize. Myers commented sadly that "many another act of swaggering folly mars for me the recollection of years which might have brought pure advance in congenial toil."[20]

Along with a certain disappointment in himself while in Hellenism's thrall, a trip to Greece in 1864 ended that period of Myers' life. "The classics," he concluded, "drew from me and fostered evil as well as good; they might aid imaginative impulse and detachment from sordid interests, but they had no check for lust and pride."[21] What he wanted, it seems, was subjective existence as rapturous as that supplied by the ancients, yet somehow more exalted, more rare, less sullied by the "common" tendencies he spent a lifetime trying to extirpate from his personality. Myers knew his inner life required tempering, and so crucial was its condition to him that he entered the first of his crisis phases. Without a more satisfying brand of inner experience, he could see himself moving into a netherworld where his very existence had almost slipped from any visceral awareness of it or even concern for it. On a trip to the United States in 1865, he impulsively swam the river below Niagara Falls at night. He later noted that this incident marked the only time in his life when the question "What if I die?" produced "an answer blank of emotion."[22]

For Myers, that state of affairs simply couldn't last. On returning to England he was elected a fellow and classical lecturer at Trinity, then fell under the influence of the alluring Josephine Butler. This extraordinary woman was adept at what has been called "the spiritual seduction" of young men, and she succeeded in imparting to Myers her own perfervid brand of Christianity. In a typical appraisal, Myers declared that Butler offered not Christianity's externals, not its "encumbering forms and dogmas," but rather "its heart of fire."[23]

But this attempted regeneration of the richness and intensity of his subjective experience, for which Myers quite literally lived, did not withstand the onslaught of Victorian science. Myers' interest in science carves out for him a distinctive place in the mystical tradition to which his consuming passion for the inner life attaches him. An admittedly self-taught amateur, he was to gain some measure of scientific sophistication as the years went by. Even by 1869, he was sufficiently versed in the scientific thought of his day to have experienced a profound disillusionment with his own beliefs. It can easily be imagined that the agnosticism in which he floated until 1873 would be, for Myers, "a dull pain borne with joyless doggedness, sometimes flashed into a horror of reality that made the world spin before one's eyes."[24] Myers seems to have been a man who actually tried to experience—not just believe in, but experience—numinous reality. Losing his conviction that such experience was really afforded by the universe, now or eternally, was shattering.

He resigned from the university and affiliated himself with the movement for the higher education of women, where he became close to Henry and Eleanor Sidgwick. But this brief and atypical spurt of social involvement could not compensate for what had been lost. He became an inspector of schools, eventually supporting himself in that capacity in the Cambridge district. But it is difficult to imagine him doing anything but going through the motions of his occupation. Agnosticism for Myers was a suffocating prison. His autobiography speaks bitterly of that period as one of "scorn of human life, of anger at destiny, of cynical preference of the pleasures of the passing hour."[25] His old terror of death returned in force. In fact, he must have felt very much like a walking corpse.

Ironically, the scientific perspective that had deprived him of his spirituality offered an escape route. He became part of his friend Sidgwick's circle during its early explorations into Spiritualism. While initially unenthusiastic toward so baldly empirical a brand of faith ("reentering by the scullery window that heavenly mansion out of which I had been kicked through the front door"[26]), he became optimistic about the idea of locating through scientific observation the immortal, ineffable aspect of existence.

Myers' romantic liaison with Annie Marshall undoubtedly sharpened his enthusiasm for the sort of work Sidgwick was undertaking. Annie, the unhappy wife of one of Myers' own cousins, channeled their relationship in a platonic direction, and Myers found the experience wondrous. It convinced him that there was indeed something simultaneously rapturous and imperishable in existence, something "that was striving upwards into life divine." His love for Annie Marshall provided the experience of the ineffable that he had always craved. It was as passionate as Hellenism and Butlerized Christianity had been, yet it was less sullied by egoism and sensuality than Hellenism, and it was sufficiently intense to promise the immortality Christianity could not persuasively argue.[27]

When Annie died, Myers was desolate. On Sidgwick's advice he married in 1880 and eventually sired three children (whom he barely mentions in his autobiography). But the formation of the S.P.R. proved the really effective compensation for his loss. Myers believed that the sort of love he had known was one indication of a whole level of existence—an unquenchable, spiritual vitalism—that a scientific perspective, properly applied, must necessarily illuminate rather than deny. And so F. W. H. Myers, "amateur poet and self-taught *savant,*" came to the field of psychical research intent on uncovering in its entirety the stratum of existence he felt he had already glimpsed. The gateway to it, he hoped, was somewhere in "non-material mind." If he could find it, he wanted deeply to share awareness of it with his entire society. "I want to snatch our young Ray-Lankesters as brands from the burning," he said, "to save the men who associate religion and the mad-house, psychology and the vivisection table, Love and the Strand."[28]

By the time of his death he was convinced he had succeeded. This was in part the result of work undertaken by his friend, Edmund Gurney.

Gurney shared a great deal with Myers, particularly the emphasis on a highly subjective sentience as life's most compelling range of experience. He was, if anything, even more concerned than Myers that contemporary British culture might erase the richness and passion of the inner life, and he fought with something approaching desperation to prevent it. Like Myers, he sought not to subvert or wreck the scientific *weltanschauung* but rather to expand it so that it might encompass and acknowledge the legitimacy of a metaphysical perspective. In both his curiously antimaterialistic scientism and his realization of the social ramifications possibly attendant upon the death of the soul, he was akin to Sidgwick. For a while, Gurney provided the cutting edge of the Cambridge group's work in psychical research, but his tortured personal history set him apart from even his closest colleagues. In the history of psychical research, he occupies a special niche all his own.

Gurney was born in 1847 in Hersham, Surrey. His father had departed from a traditional family orientation toward the legal profession and entered the church, eventually becoming a prebendary of St. Paul's. Edmund was educated in Blackheath, then Trinity College, Cambridge. But although his ability as a classical scholar was sufficient to earn him a fellowship at Trinity in 1872, his major interest during his youth and early manhood was music. [29] He was intent on becoming skilled in both performance and composition, and studied music for three years at Harrow.

Gurney was a striking man, both physically and intellectually. But it was his misfortune to pursue careers in those areas where his gifts were inadequate. Music was one of them. His realization of his own mediocrity undoubtedly contributed to the melancholia that would become a permanent and at times debilitating feature of his personality. His failures seem to have catalyzed in him a certain passion that would never relinquish its hold. For the rest of his life, Gurney would be acutely aware of the gap between the complex texture of inner, subjective, emotional experience—like the appreciation of music—and the formalized, standardized forms of recognition and channels of expression afforded it by the external world. A man of extremely keen sensibilities, Gurney was in fact grieved by a deep sense of loss at what he considered to be the disjuncture between the two. He never gave up trying to recast in more generous form the channels offered by the world for the operations of intensely subjective, personalized feeling.

Part of what was entailed in this quest, and what both Gurney and Myers meant by "the inner life," can be gleaned from a careful reading of Gurney's book *The Power of Sound*. In that work he attempted to impart greater amplitude to formal musical criticism's understanding of excellence. He began by trying to define musical form, which he concluded was properly located in the sequential progress from one tone, chord, or motif to the next. Then he went on to warn that formal design alone may provide a means for locating a particular piece among the categories of musical expressions, but not for appraising its merits. ("It is nothing in favour of any piece that the mechanical part of it, the skeleton, so to speak, places it under one head or another.")[30] Rather, the details presented within that form, the melodic "bits" of any composition, were the key to its success. And ultimate judgment on their quality was, to Gurney, unconditionally intuitive. ("Whatever explanations of musical effect turn out to be possible, the exercise of the musical faculty will present an ultimately inexplicable element.")[31] In his book, Gurney explicitly treated musical appreciation as one aspect of that mysterious "inner life," the vitality of which he was so intent on protecting and, indeed, promoting. He stated that the musical sensibility "condenses a very large amount of inner life . . . into a very brief span of actual time," giving sensory reality to emotions that "lie in a region where thought and language struggle to penetrate."[32]

In 1875, the nature of Gurney's own inner life was significantly colored by a family tragedy. Three of his sisters, to whom he was very close, died in a boating accident on the Nile. From this point on, Gurney's cast of mind darkened considerably. His already sharp sensitivity to pain became obsessive, and he told William James that "the mystery of the Universe and the indefensibility of human suffering" were never far from him.[33] A desire to probe that mystery may have motivated his next career choice, medicine. In 1877 he began a course of medical studies at University College, London, and completed them at Cambridge. His second M.B. was obtained there in 1880, and the next stop was St. George's Hospital, for clinical training. But Gurney was, apparently, simply incapable of living with what he found there.[34] He considered hospital conditions deplorable, and abandoned medicine forthwith. Married shortly before his experience at St.

George's, his need to find some satisfying career became pressing. He turned to law, but was unable to sustain any real commitment to it.

Gurney's problem, it would seem, was that none of the ways in which the world addressed human suffering, either culturally (via religion) or institutionally (via the medical and legal professions) could satisfactorily encompass its magnitude as he himself so viscerally felt it. Gurney in fact defected from the camp of religious orthodoxy precisely because his understanding of suffering precluded any possibility of a benign deity. But while his sense of the omnipresence of pain wrecked for him the viability of religious formulae, he could not consider what he knew of the world's responses to the problem—rationalized law and bureaucratized medicine—adequate substitutes. His temperament was such that the process of actually categorizing and quantifying pain, crucial to the marshaling of worldly resources to deal with it, somehow violated his sense of its cosmic, organic reality, somehow appeared to him only trivial ameliorations or even ignoble exploitations of that oppressively immanent reality.[35]

Gurney's feelings in this regard are perhaps best illustrated by his involvement in the vivisection controversy. In papers on the subject, he questioned the "utilitarian" provivisection argument, which of course held that experiments on animals would benefit a more precious species, man. Gurney felt that attempting to discriminate tolerable from intolerable brands of pain-infliction opened a Pandora's box of logical and moral problems. While by no means a fanatical antivivisectionist, he feared the blurring or dulling of our awareness of pain. He insisted on the retention of an emotional, personal, subjective response to it, as opposed to a calculation based on dubious standards of objectivity.[36]

In this as in all else, Gurney, like Myers, was a champion and protector of the inner life. That his own came to be dominated by considerations of suffering in no way detracted from his demand that the world recognize if not the inner man's autonomy then at least his reality. Like Myers, when Sidgwick assumed the presidency of the

S.P.R. Gurney became an enthusiastic member. Psychical research seemed to afford an excellent opportunity for investigating and perhaps in a sense celebrating "inner man" himself. Gurney threw himself into the S.P.R.'s work with even more relish than his friend, possibly out of the sheer joy of finding labor that suited his interests and values so perfectly. With Myers, he was to become the Society's principal investigator. With Myers, he was to fashion psychical research into something quite distinct from orthodox Spiritualism. It was to be not a verification of the spirits without, but an homage to the ineffable within.

NOTES

1. W. H. Salter, *The Society for Psychical Research* (London: The Society for Psychical Research, 1970), p. 9.

2. *Light,* vol. 13 (September 9, 1883), pp. 429–30.

The January 9, 1893, edition of *Light* contained Rogers' full account of the origins and early days of the S.P.R., including his own intentions.

3. Arthur and Eleanor Sidgwick, *Henry Sidgwick: A Memoir* (London: Macmillan, 1906), pp. 33–38, 198–202.

4. Henry Sidgwick, *The Methods of Ethics,* 7th ed. (Chicago: University of Chicago Press, 1962).

5. See C. D. Broad's *Religion, Philosophy, and Psychical Research* (New York: Harcourt, Brace, 1953). See also Gauld, *The Founders of Psychical Research,* pp. 136–42.

6. See Turner's "The Pursuit of Complex Wisdom" in *Between Science and Religion* for a fine treatment of Sidgwick's ideas and motivations.

7. Minutes of those meetings, and of all meetings of the Society's governing council after it was officially established, are kept in the archives of the Society for Psychical Research in London.

8. Rogers' account of the S.P.R.'s formation in the January 9, 1893, edition of *Light* contains a discussion of early Spiritualist support for the Society, with the notable exception of William Stainton Moses.

9. An important council function was the screening and recruitment of members, especially the recruitment of important intellectual figures. Among those immediately enlisted were Charles Dodgson (better known as "Lewis

Carroll"), John Ruskin, and Alfred Lord Tennyson. Either the council or the president also convened general meetings (Minutes, June 15, 1882).

10. The S.P.R. was to be funded by subscription fees and private donations. The council reserved the exclusive right to authorize each specific expenditure by any investigating committee, rather than devolving a set sum on the committees and letting them spend it freely. Committees were to keep records of their own meetings, including attendance reports, for the council. From their work, the council was to select papers to be read at general meetings of the Society (while also deciding which reporters and outside observers were to be invited to those general meetings). The council would also select the papers to be published in the S.P.R.'s official organ, the *Proceedings of the Society for Psychical Research*. The *Proceedings* were to be issued first to S.P.R. members. Then they would be collected in yearly or biyearly volumes for distribution to such booksellers, libraries, learned societies, and other groups as the council chose (Minutes, June 15, 1882).

11. Circular "On the General Work of the Society," reprinted in the *Proceedings*, vol. 1 (1882–83), p. 296.

12. Ibid., p. 300.

13. Baron Carl von Reichenbach was a Moravian industrialist with a taste for chemical research. Through it, he became interested in mesmerism. In the 1840s he had argued that patients he observed being treated by a Viennese surgeon were able to detect a visual luminosity around magnetic poles, and sometimes around crystals and even the human body. He decided that this luminosity, which he named the "odyle," must be an unknown force related to magnetism, which certain sensitives were able to discern (Inglis, *Natural and Supernatural*, p. 183).

14. See Gauld, *The Founders of Psychical Research*, pp. 137–53; and Salter, *The Society for Psychical Research*, pp. 7–8.

15. F.W.H. Myers, *Fragments of Inner Life* (London: The Society for Psychical Research, 1961), p. 6. In 1893, Myers printed at his own expense a few copies of this intimate autobiography, which he circulated to his closest friends. In 1961, sixty years after his death, the S.P.R. followed his instructions and published a limited public edition. There is a copy in the archives of the S.P.R. in London.

16. Ibid., p. 8.

17. Ibid., p. 8.

18. Ibid., p. 10.

19. Ibid., p. 9.

20. Ibid., p. 9.

21. Ibid., p. 10.

22. Ibid., p. 12.

23. Gauld, *The Founders of Psychical Research,* p. 95; and Myers, *Fragments,* p. 13.

24. Myers, *Fragments,* p. 14.

25. Ibid., p. 36.

26. Ibid., p. 15.

27. Ibid., pp. 16–28; Gauld, *The Founders of Psychical Research,* pp. 116–24; Turner, *Between Science and Religion,* p. 112.

28. Quoted in Turner, *Between Science and Religion,* p. 116.

29. For biographical data on Gurney, see the *Dictionary of National Biography* (Oxford, 1917); Gauld, *The Founders of Psychical Research,* pp. 154–82; and Edward T. Cone's introduction to Gurney's own *The Power of Sound* (New York and London: Basic Books, 1966; first published in 1880).

30. Gurney, *The Power of Sound,* p. 100.

31. Ibid., p. 86.

32. Ibid., pp. 347–48.

33. Quoted in Gauld, *The Founders of Psychical Research,* p. 156.

34. Ibid., p. 156.

35. Ibid., pp. 153–86.

36. See Gurney's "A Chapter on the Ethics of Pain," *Fortnightly Review,* vol. 36 (1881), pp. 778–96; and his "An Epilogue on Vivisection," *Cornhill Magazine,* vol. 45 (1882), pp. 191–99.

Chapter Four

The Transmutation of the Spiritualist Impulse: The S.P.R., 1882–1886

METHODS AND PROCEDURES

As an intellectual discipline, psychical research began as a rather amorphous inquiry into the equally amorphous subject of nonmaterial mind.[1] Its practitioners had an organizational structure within which to work, and a general idea of the phenomena they wanted to investigate. But, as in any intellectual discipline, questions of methods and procedures had to be addressed before the practitioners could actually yield any output. In this case, the problems were particularly thorny. In resolving them, the psychical researchers enclosed themselves in a methodological framework that determined both the specific range of phenomena they would approach and the analytical perspectives they could employ. In this manner they began the vital task of hammering a vague research consideration into a body of work with a recognizable form, and message, for the public.

The questions of methods and procedures were raised in an exchange that occurred in the pages of *The Nineteenth Century* shortly after the S.P.R. was organized. Gurney and Myers had joined Barrett on the thought transference committee, and the three of them made the first public presentation of psychical research to the outside world in the June 1882 issue of the aforementioned review. Their article on "Thought Transference" described for the most part experiments the three had undertaken with the Creery children. It began by announcing the experimenters' realization that any individual attempting to divine someone else's thoughts in "supersensuous" fashion might be guided by subtle muscular, tactile, or auditory clues. These, the investigators acknowledged, would be faint but nonetheless entirely orthodox examples of the processing of information by the senses. Startling results obtained with the girls in the presence of family members were dismissed on precisely those grounds. But the psychical researchers went on to claim that the Creery children had still succeeded in guessing names, playing cards, and hidden objects known only to the experimenters themselves with a rate of success above the level of chance. Barrett, Gurney, and Myers insisted that they had imparted no clues. They advanced the hypothesis that the children's minds had actually received data with no transmission from the senses.

Horatio Donkin, Ray-Lankester's associate in the Slade trial, replied immediately. Regarding the psychical researchers' assertion that they themselves had given the children no sensory clues, Donkin noted that "in all scientific inquiries the good faith of individuals concerned should form no part of the data on which the conclusion is to rest."[2] He pointed out that the children had not been blindfolded, nor had silence been preserved. The girls, in fact, had been told when they were mistaken and allowed to try again. Since sensory clues, even if unlikely, were still possible, Donkin dismissed the entire set of experiments. He cautioned that "common sense demands that every known mode of explanation be exhausted before the possibility of an unknown mode is considered."

Donkin's criticism had emphasized the scientific dictum that extraordinary claims require extraordinary evidence. As Sidgwick and the Cambridge group realized, the claim that the Creery children's minds had received images without mediation by the senses was indeed an extraordinary one. The problem was deciding what exactly could be held to constitute extraordinary evidence for that claim. This, the S.P.R.'s leaders knew, was more than a methodological problem related to one specific investigation. It was the pivotal methodological-cum-procedural problem for psychical research itself. The whole notion that some portion of human mental activity was completely independent of physiological matter, which the S.P.R. was committed to analyzing, was in its entirety an extraordinary claim. Without some sort of resolution to this question of appropriate evidence, the inquiry simply could not proceed. The manner in which the question was resolved would determine what the actual content of psychical research was to be. By the time the S.P.R. held its first general meeting on July 17, 1882, in London, procedural guidelines had in fact been mapped out. They were disclosed in Sidgwick's presidential address.

Sidgwick began his speech by assuring S.P.R. members (and whatever outside observers were present) of the Society's corporate impartiality regarding the authenticity of the phenomena that were to be investigated. The S.P.R.'s purpose, he said, was only to illuminate subjects that professional scientists had unjustifiably ignored. "Regarded as a Society, we are quite unpledged," said Sidgwick, "and as individuals, we are all agreed that any particular investigation that we may make should be carried on with a single-minded desire to ascertain the facts, and without any foregone conclusion as to their nature."[3] But, having just described the S.P.R. as an independent investigative body with no "foregone conclusion," Sidgwick's subsequent discussion of central steering policy was explicitly presented as a set of strategic and tactical guidelines for combating scientific skepticism:

> We must not expect any decisive effect in the direction at which we primarily aim, on the common sense of mankind, from any single piece of evidence, however complete it has been made. Scientific incredulity has been so long in growing, and has so many and so strong roots, that we shall only kill it, if we are able to kill it at all as regards any of those questions, by burying it alive under a heap of facts. . . . We must accumulate fact upon fact, and add experiment upon experiment, and, I should say, not wrangle too much with incredulous outsiders about the conclusiveness of any one, but trust to the mass of evidence for conviction.[4]

Actually, the grand strategy of the S.P.R.'s probe into nonmaterial mind had already been manifested in the eclectic demarcation of research zones to be investigated by the committees. In their organization's very structure, psychical researchers had shown they would not look to any single phenomenon to demonstrate nonmaterial mind, but rather to a whole range of them. Regarding the presentation of their case to scientists and the general public, this emphasis on the sheer bulk of evidence was repeated. Just as nonmaterial mind was to be demonstrated not by thought transference alone but by thought transference in connection with a wide range of other phenomena, so were thought transference and all other selected phenomena to be demonstrated not by one experiment but by an accumulation of them. That, to the psychical researchers, would constitute "extraordinary evidence."[5] As for the validity of each single experiment, they would take whatever measures they could to ensure proper test conditions. Beyond that, they had only one response to Donkin's reminder that the "good faith" of investigators could not be invoked to lend credence to experimental findings. Sidgwick explained:

> We have done all that we can when the critic has nothing left to allege except that the investigator is in the trick. . . .
> We must drive the objector into the position of being forced either to admit the phenomena as inexplicable, at least by him, or to accuse the investigators either of lying or cheating or of a blindness or forgetfulness incompatible with any intellectual condition except absolute idiocy.[6]

Sidgwick felt it was important to establish the hard-headedness, the insusceptibility to illusion, of psychical researchers themselves. That consideration probably had much to do with the way he planned to treat Spiritualist phenomena. He felt that paid, professional mediums as a group had already demonstrated great skills at defrauding intelligent people. ("I think that even educated and scientific Spiritualists were not quite prepared for the amount of fraud which has recently come to light.")[7] Tactically, he felt it would be best to steer clear of them entirely. He therefore explained to the Society's predominantly Spiritualist membership that professional mediums would be ignored, for the most part, in psychical research. While declining to lay down any "hard and fast rule" against the use of paid mediums, Sidgwick explained that in general the Society would address itself to "phenomena where no ordinary motives of fraud—at any rate I may say, no pecuniary motives—can come in."[8]

With the elaboration of a central steering policy to deal with the issue of evidence, Sidgwick in a sense had completed a set of formal and informal screening mechanisms within the S.P.R. through which his and other individuals' essentially philosophical concern with nonmaterial mind would be processed into the actual content of psychical research. Those screening mechanisms included the original demarcation of areas to be investigated; the composition of the investigating corps; and the emphasis on volume of material and deemphasis of the best-known phenomena of Spiritualism (i.e., those associated with professional mediumship). The studies that would be read or published as examples of psychical research, the actual substance of the discipline as it was to be presented to the public, would usually begin in the investigating committees (where professional mediumship would be dismissed), then be fashioned by members of the Cambridge group (especially Gurney and Myers), either on the committees or in the council, to emphasize the sheer quantity of evidence. The visible shape psychical research was beginning to take was reflected in the first report of the committee on thought-reading, read after Sidgwick's speech at that first general meeting.

That report, written by Barrett, Gurney, and Myers, constituted their response to Donkin's criticism. In it, the psychical researchers categorized the types of data they had collected in more than a year's work with the Creery children and others, begun before the S.P.R. had even been inaugurated. They attached varying degrees of weight or importance to each type by virtue of the stringency of experimental controls used in gathering it. For example, when the hands or eyes of the investigator were in contact with the subject the results of thought-reading efforts, however striking impressionistically, were acknowledged as providing in no formal sense sufficient evidence of any mental capacity outside already recognized ones. Where the possibility of unconscious clues had been ruled out by various means, successful results were held to be of something like "moderate" weight (subjects were still occasionally successful, but neither success nor failure could be correlated to any experimental variable). Finally, reference was made to cases collected by the literary committee where similar thoughts and sensations were alleged to have occurred in minds separated by great distances. In the S.P.R. experimenters' view, this provided an additional and quite strong suggestion that some unrecognized mental property might accrue to at least some individuals. According to the authors, the result of this compilation of evidence of varying degrees of quality was that, while none was in itself completely persuasive, taken as a whole it promised that "further advances along the lines of research here indicated may, and we believe will, necessitate a modification of that general view of the relation of mind to matter to which modern science has long been gravitating."[9]

This report represented in microcosm the *modus operandi* of psychical research as a discipline: the accumulation of material on given phenomena in volume, until some general picture emerged. The course had been set for the intellectual adventure psychical research represented.

THE TELEPATHIC DIMENSION AND ITS MANIFESTATIONS

For the next several months, the S.P.R.'s principal investigators groped toward that general picture. When the S.P.R. held its second general meeting on December 9, 1882, its members were given a somewhat clearer delineation of what the new discipline they were subsidizing was really saying. Sidgwick began the meeting by noting that some of the criticisms already leveled at the new Society's work bore a suspicious resemblance to clerical defenses of dogma in earlier times.[10] Then, after reiterating the Society's chosen means of dealing with those criticisms ("if a dozen [experiments] will not do, let us give them a score"), he called on representatives of the various committees to describe the fruits of their labors to date.

Some reports were disappointing. The Reichenbach committee regretfully announced that its work had been delayed by unexplained "preliminary difficulties." The haunted house committee reported little beyond the methodological dictum that no single witness's evidence would provide satisfactory data for its investigation. The thought transference committee, however, had remained very active. It reported that further experiments with the Creery children showed that, while their success rate was still above what chance alone should have supplied, the children were gradually losing their powers. But at the same time, the committee had found by casting its nets further afield that the same capacity was present in a far larger number of persons than had been supposed. It had solicited data from both S.P.R. members and the general public, via newspaper advertisements, for example. From the unexpectedly large pool of talent discovered, another gem had emerged. Douglas Blackburn, a Brighton journalist, had brought to the committee's attention the remarkable results in thought reading or "will-impression" he had had with a Brighton stage mesmerist named G. A. Smith. Gurney and Myers had investigated Smith. They found him able to go beyond the level of card guessing into the reproduction while blindfolded of drawings Blackburn made, and even the experience of similar sensations when Gurney and Myers "pinched or otherwise hurt" the journalist.[11] And as the thought transference committee moved beyond the Creery children, psychical research moved beyond thought transference.

The literary committee, with Gurney and Myers its driving forces, had been enormously industrious. In addition to supplementing the work of the thought transference and all other committees, it had undertaken a project all its own. It had collected both historical data and wholly new testimony on all the Society's chosen fields of interest and tried to find some general interpretive canopy or conceptual overview under which all might be subsumed. The committee held the new testimony to be, naturally, the more reliable. It had elicited that testimony via circulars sent to friends as well as to London and provincial journals, and considered it relatively strong because some precautions had been taken against hoax and exaggeration. The committee had accepted only those cases where confirmation was available to the effect that either the phenomenon witnessed had been seen by more than one person or the phenomenon, if an entirely subjective "impression," palpably resembled some real event or object of which the witness could have had no conscious knowledge.

Gurney and Myers had been deeply impressed by the Creery and, especially, the Smith-Blackburn experiments. On that basis, they decided to treat their new data as though intentional thought transference were a solidly established fact, in order to see how much of it that fact as then understood could explain. They began with a breakdown of simple, willful thought transference into its component variables. These included the presence of "agent" and "percipient"; the "normal condition" of each; and the transfer of impressions without apparent exercise of the senses. New cases collected by the literary committee were then classified in terms of deviation from those norms. For example, instances were found where either agent or percipient was in an "abnormal" state (dreaming, entranced, ill, near death); where both were in abnormal states; where each was in a different abnormal state. Thus far, the literary committee had not gone beyond the normalcy variable, but it was already prepared to suggest that "thought transference" was not an adequate term or an adequate concept to cover those actions of the mind unrelated to the processing of data through the senses. The committee's conclusion was exciting:

> The analogy of Thought-transference, which seemed to offer such a convenient logical start, cannot be pressed too far. Our phenomena break through any attempt to group them under heads of transferred impression; and we venture to introduce the words *Telœsthesia* and *Telepathy* to cover all cases of impression received at a distance without the normal operation of the recognised sense organs. [12]

What Gurney and Myers were announcing was that thought

transference, as had been hoped, was merely the tip of the iceberg. A whole range of phenomena was occurring, indicating that thought transference was not some highly singular gift possessed by certain unusual individuals. Rather, it appeared to be only one property of an entire aspect of mental life, hitherto uninvestigated yet possessed by some undetermined percentage of the population. Gurney and Myers were submitting that the direct action of the mind, unassisted by physiological agencies, existed in many forms with myriad nuances and variations. There was some special faculty within the human organism, some capacity of which the deliberate transfer of ideas was only one part. They called that faculty "telepathy": a wholly unexplored dimension of mental activity.

The notion of "telepathy" was to provide a conceptual overview for the entire field of psychical research. "Nonmaterial mind" had been a philosophical postulate. "Telepathy" was essentially the same idea, but related to research rather than philosophy. Gurney and Myers were trying to derive it from research findings; and, more to the point, they wanted to use it as an interpretive framework for subsequent research. Finding the locus of its manifestations, explicating its qualities completely, even perhaps locating the source of its energies: these, for Gurney and Myers, would be the real stuff of psychical research. With the concept of "telepathy" or "telepathic mind" they in effect gave psychical research something to research, as opposed to a philosophical position to argue deductively. The actual content of the discipline would consist largely of an attempt to deepen the original, primitive understanding of telepathy that was presented in the literary committee's report at the S.P.R.'s second general meeting. It could hardly have been coincidental that it was Gurney and Myers, with their commitment to preserving the richness and texture of the inner life, who originally formulated the idea of telepathy and who would be most active in exploring it. Telepathic mind promised to reveal forms of sensation, will, and cerebral experience in general of which even they had scarcely dreamed.

The substance of psychical research under the new (or the old, newly described) interpretive canopy of telepathy was amply demonstrated in the S.P.R. *Proceedings* and general meetings over the next year. Phenomena that the Society's principal investigators thought could be understood as manifestations of telepathic mind pretty much circumscribed their subject matter. Considerations of them (almost always by members of the Cambridge group, especially Gurney and Myers) dominated the S.P.R.'s research output.

Chief among these research topics was mesmerism. Edmund Gurney was so interested in it that he took on the chairmanship of the committee on mesmerism in addition to his other duties. Gurney, in fact, saw mesmerism as the possible key to unlocking the entire scope and genesis of telepathic mind. His committee concerned itself largely with the virtuoso G. A. Smith, this time in Smith's capacity as a mesmerist.[13] Gurney found that Smith could directly transmit a suggestion to certain entranced people that would be operationalized upon their return to normalcy. He could also induce both local and general anesthesia. Most interesting, however, was his ability to transfer a physical sensation from his own person to the entranced person without direct sensory contact. Since Smith had earlier shown his own ability to experience the physical sensations of another in the thought transference experiments, the notion that he was also capable of imparting those sensations to someone in a trance state tantalized Gurney. Perhaps he had found an individual who possessed the mysterious "effluence" mesmerists had spoken of forty years earlier. In those days, the trance state had been induced by "passes" (dramatic movements of the hands or eyes), by which it was alleged that the strange force of "animal magnetism" or the "effluence" was transmitted. Gurney thought that the effluence might actually be telepathic mind in some extremely heightened form, and that the trance state might be the means of getting at the source of telepathic energy itself.

He was encouraged in these speculations by what seemed to be a whole recasting of scholarly thought on mesmerism on the Continent. The term "mesmerism" had actually been out of vogue for over a generation. Induction of the trance state was usually termed "hypnotism," reflecting the belief that trances were of entirely physiological origin. But in the early 1880s, that belief was not as unanimous as it had been earlier.

In the 1850s, the Scottish surgeon James Braid had found that trances could be induced with a minimum of histrionics. All that was required was getting the subject to stare at a bright object a little above the eye line. This meant that trance-casting involved no unfathomable effluence emanating from fingertips or eyeballs, but rather a normal if delicate physiological reaction. [14]

Mesmerists had claimed that a whole host of "higher phenomena," clairvoyance and even omniscience, occurred in the trance state. But Braid argued that while the "mesmerized" were often capable of remarkable feats (like describing the shape of an object held behind the head), these reflected not supernatural attributes but the functioning of the senses in extremely exalted states. Where there had once been clairvoyance, Braid had substituted hyperacuity of the senses; and from the sideshows of mesmerism had emerged the analyzable phenomenon of hypnotism.

The study progressed further on the Continent. By the 1880s, the German physiologist Rudolf Heidenhain was presenting hypnotism as "an inhibition of the action of the ganglion cells of the cerebral cortex, induced by continued weak stimulation of other nerves." [15] Jean-Martin Charcot at the Salpêtrière in Paris took Heidenhain's analysis a step further. Charcot experimented with "Braidism" on diagnosed hysterics and found a remarkable similarity in the appearance of cataleptic and somnambulistic states. He also discovered that nonhysterics under hypnosis demonstrated again and again the classic symptoms of hysteria (e.g., the "rainbow," where a patient's body stiffens into an arc). His conclusion was that hypnosis was simply "hystero-epilepsy artificially induced" by a form of "neuro-muscular excitability." [16] In his lectures to the Academy in 1882, Charcot announced that not only had hypnosis proved to be the neurological condition Heidenhain had described, but that this neurological condition was the key to hysteria. Henceforth, hypnosis could be studied as a manifestation of the latter pathology.

But Charcot's analysis spawned a revisionist school. In 1882, a Dr. Liébeault cured a patient whom Hippolyte Bernheim of the clinic at Nancy had treated unsuccessfully for years. When Bernheim visited Liébeault, he found the latter able to derive therapy rather than hysteria from the trance state. Bernheim introduced hypnotherapy into his own hospital and concluded that Charcot was mistaken in his analysis of the physiological mechanisms by which hypnosis worked. While Charcot went on to form a *Société de Psychologie Physiologique* in the belief that psychology was best approached via neurophysiology, Bernheim's "Nancy school" held that the physiological route was not illuminated by the facts of hypnotism in the way Charcot thought. Whatever hypnotism was, Bernheim felt, it was not hysteria pure and simple, and it was not neurologically generated. Dr. Liébeault went so far as to contend that there was indeed some evidence for the "higher phenomena" of mesmerism.[17] In so doing, he associated the Nancy school with the position that there might be something to the effluence after all. Relating his work to these developments, Edmund Gurney announced in the summer of 1883 that the S.P.R.'s mesmeric committee had established a strong prima facie case for the reality of mesmeric, as opposed to hypnotic, phenomena (although final confirmation awaited further experimentation).[18]

Throughout the late months of 1883, the Society's *Proceedings* were filled with articles supplementing and expanding existing data on mesmerism and the now familiar subject of thought transference.[19] Council meetings of the period were largely concerned with editing, publishing, and disseminating those findings as effectively as possible.[20] Behind the scenes, plans were underway for bringing another range of phenomena within the interpretive framework of the "telepathic mind."

Gurney and Myers, armed with data from the literary committee and the now-defunct haunted house committee, had become interested in "apparitions," or appearances of the form of someone on the point of death to individuals who were far away from and/or unaware of the condition of the person whose wraith they saw. The researchers' plan for investigating apparitions was presented both to the Society (at the general meeting of March 28, 1884) and, a little later, to the general public (in the May 1884 edition of *The Nineteenth Century*). The psychical researchers were theoretically prepared to consider apparitions purely subjective experiences, or hallucinations, with no objective, nonmental reality. But they argued that only the collection of a sufficient number of cases in sufficiently well-documented detail would tell whether or not the coincidence of the percipient's hallucination with his acquaintance's death crisis was solely a function of chance. If not, they claimed, then apparitions were more likely to be hallucinations directly caused by consciously or unconsciously applied telepathic force.[21]

Actually, by the time "Apparitions" was published in *The Nineteenth Century,* Gurney and Myers had already concluded that their hypothesis was fundamentally correct.[22] But to dismiss the case for random or acausal hallucination they had to demonstrate that the percentage of the general public experiencing "crisis-apparitions" was significantly above the chance factor. That, in turn, would require some determination of the numerical incidence of such experiences that the general public, minus chronic hallucinators, could be expected to generate randomly, as well as some determination of their real numerical incidence. Naturally, to achieve these calculations a formidable data-collection process loomed. Questionnaires had to be assembled and cases collected in enormous bulk. But the challenge was accepted in the hope that this approach to apparitions, "the standing jest and standing mystery of every age," would conclusively reveal "phantasms of the living" to be yet another projection from that wondrous region, the telepathic mind. Myers and particularly Gurney, while continuing their work on mesmerism, threw themselves wholeheartedly into the new task.

By the close of 1884, the S.P.R. was expanding its organizational activities in other ways. First and foremost, Barrett had succeeded in interesting some American thinkers in psychical research during a tour of the United States, and plans were underway for the sister society that would be inaugurated there in January 1885. Also, a new serial publication had been added to the *Proceedings*. *The Journal of the Society for Psychical Research* was to consist of cases of psychical phenomena sent to the investigating committees by members who specifically wanted them recorded. These would be sifted and edited by the president and the S.P.R.'s newly created honorary secretary (Gurney), then printed and circulated to members free of charge. In addition, Richard Hodgson (of the Cambridge group) had been dispatched to India at Sidgwick's personal expense to report on the marvels associated with the colorful Madame Blavatsky and her Theosophical movement.[23]

All in all, an air of confident vitality seems to have characterized the S.P.R.'s officers and active workers at this early stage of its history. But the Spiritualists, psychical research's presumed constituency and certainly the S.P.R.'s major membership bloc, were not feeling very confident at all.

THE DEFECTION OF THE SPIRITUALISTS

Almost from the Society's inception, there seems to have been a certain restiveness among Spiritualists regarding the S.P.R. and psychical research. The Spiritualist E. Dawson Rogers had helped organize the Society in the explicit hope that it would help legitimate Spiritualism scientifically. Yet as early as February 3, 1883, Rogers had found it necessary to reply in the pages of *Light* to what were apparently some rather pointed inquiries from Spiritualists about the S.P.R.'s actual yield.

> A correspondent asks, "What is the distinction between the Society for Psychical Research and the Central Association of Spiritualists?" and also inquires whether there is any antagonism between the two bodies. . . .

There is a sharp line of distinction between the S.P.R. and the Central Association of Spiritualists. The Spiritualists have a settled faith—nay, more, a certain knowledge—in regard to facts about which the S.P.R. would not profess to have any knowledge whatever. The S.P.R. are busy with phenomena only, seeking evidence of their existence, but not yet hazarding even a hint of their spiritual origin. To them the idea of spirit-communion, of sweet converse with dear departed friends—so precious to Spiritualists—has no present interest. We speak of them, of course, as a Society—not of individual members. As a Society they are studying the mere bones and muscles, and have not penetrated to the heart and soul.[24]

While noting that psychical research and Spiritualism were not exactly coterminous, Rogers went on to express the hope that psychical researchers would eventually become "Spiritualists without the Spirits, and ultimately very like other Spiritualists."

But Spiritualists within the S.P.R. were evidently becoming concerned as to what this "Spiritualism without the Spirits" really was. In a presidential address on July 18, 1883, Sidgwick had acknowledged a certain reluctance on the part of the Society's Spiritualist members to cooperate fully or involve themselves with the actual practice of psychical research. The Spiritualists, he said, had not contributed to the established investigating committees anything approaching the amount of data expected from them. Further, local investigating teams had not been organized by S.P.R. members, despite the encouragement of the council. In his gently chiding speech, Sidgwick interpreted this as an unscientific love of the mysterious, a feeling that spirit communications "should be kept as sacred mysteries and not exposed to be scrutinised in the mood of cold curiosity which they conceive to belong to science." He assured his audience that "we do not approach these matters in any light or trivial spirit," but he also insisted that the S.P.R. had to treat Spiritualist experiences "as a part of the great aggregate which we call Nature."[25]

However, spiritualist disaffection could not be handled quite so glibly. In fact, throughout 1884 there were suggestions that it was growing. Dawson Rogers attempted to resign from the council (although not from the S.P.R. entirely) in both February and October of that year. Each time, he was persuaded to stay.[26] Rogers' reasons for wanting to loosen his affiliation with the S.P.R. were not articulated. Whatever his own reasons were, the minutes of the council meetings throughout 1884 show large numbers of members tendering outright resignations from the Society. Some tension certainly was developing in the council by the end of that year, evidently between Spiritualists and the Cambridge group. In recognition of this, Sidgwick deliberately restructured the council's relationship with the committees so that the former would no longer have to endorse committee reports before they could be published.[27]

What was troubling the Spiritualists finally came out in early 1885. The catalyst was an article by Myers in the February edition of *The Contemporary Review*. In it he argued that not all cases of automatic writing were fraudulent; in some, he claimed, there was a telepathic conveyance of ideas from sitter to automatist. While finding no evidence of spirit intercourse, Myers was hopeful about what he thought automatic writing indicated about man.

> Is it not . . . at least possible that this analysis may reveal also faculties of unlooked-for range, and powers which our conscious self was not aware of possessing? . . . It seems possible that a more searching analysis of our mental constitution may reveal to us not a straitened and materialized, but a developing and expanding view of "the powers that lie folded up in man."[28]

Myers' *Contemporary Review* article explicitly reduced a particular mediumistic phenomenon, automatic writing, to an epiphenomenon of "telepathic mind." Just a short while earlier, he and Gurney had explicitly treated apparitions of the near-dead in the same way in *The Nineteenth Century*. Psychical researchers were indeed representing their field in the outside press as a probe into "the powers that lie folded up in man." But from the Spiritualist point of view, the obvious question was: what about the spirits? Psychical research was turning out to be a probe inward, deeper into the mind—not outward, toward the spirits. The S.P.R.'s Committee on the Physical Phenomena of Spiritualism had supplied absolutely nothing of what Spiritualists wanted. Sidgwick's proscription against the use of professional mediums had severely circumscribed the range of phenomena that committee would even consider investigating. In fact, it had not yet issued a major report. Immediately after Myers' *Contemporary Review* article appeared, Spiritualist impatience with the S.P.R. began to pour out. The forum for their grievances was *Light.* Dawson Rogers himself opened the floodgates when he announced in the February 14 edition: "We . . . believe the time is near at hand when the Society for Psychical Research, as a result of its investigations, will be compelled to make some distinct statement as regards 'Spiritualism.'" Rogers expressed the hope that that statement would come from an official investigation of William Eglinton, the most illustrious medium then practicing in London.

Eglinton had impressed many Spiritualist readers of *Light,* as well as members of the S.P.R. and even non-Cambridge group Society investigators. Although he was a professional, it was vigorously demanded in the March 7 edition of *Light* that he be investigated. Considerable space was given over to the Spiritualist G. D. Haughton's lambasting of the S.P.R. for the account it had given of psychical research in general, and its inattention to Eglinton in particular.

The public are apparently expected to view the phenomena almost entirely through the eyes of Messrs. Myers and Gurney, as the "Proceedings" of the Society testify. . . . We want them to come to the point, and this they steadfastly refuse to do. . . . Mr. Myers has, indeed, announced his belief in telepathy, but he still cannot believe that a spirit is at one of the poles, though telepathy between two mortals is just as mysterious and unexplainable, and even more so. . . . Still he stands shivering on the bank, and dares not take the fatal plunge—fatal as it might be to his reputation for good sense, at least among materialists.

His yoke-fellow, Mr. Gurney, appears to me in much the same plight. . . .

> And now about Mr. Eglinton. Is it not passing strange that a society which professes to investigate the claims of Spiritualism, yet neglects (may we say refuses?) to test the pretensions of Mr. Eglinton? He is a medium of world-wide celebrity. He is in London, and Messrs. Myers and Gurney, the two eyes through which the Society sees, are also in London. . . .
>
> What is the reason? I believe there is nothing they dread so much as to be forced to decide and to proclaim their decision. . . . The Society by so acting frustrates the very object of its existence.[29]

Rogers diplomatically softened the tone of the criticism in a personal response to the letter, explaining his reason for raising the subject of the S.P.R.'s lack of activity on Spiritualism. ("All we wished to say was, that . . . willingly or not, they would be compelled to answer the question—What are the points of difference and agreement between your Society and its conclusions and Spiritualism?") But he didn't hesitate to offer the pages of *Light* as a sounding board for pointed Spiritualist attacks on the S.P.R.

From those attacks it was clear that many Spiritualists felt the notion of telepathic mind to be an inadequate substitute for the spirits themselves. For Spiritualists, telepathic mind seems to have been entirely too much a phenomenon of this world, too loosely connected (if connected at all) to the idea of post-mortem existence. For them, that question of post-mortem existence was the only really significant one, the only conceivable confirmation of noumenal selfhood. Psychical research seemed to be shelving it. In the March 14, 1885, issue of *Light* Rogers gave the entire front page over to a letter on the Society's shortcomings by an anonymous Spiritualist. "X." began his letter with the observation that "telepathy is a word adopted by the leaders of the Society for Psychical Research as one which expresses the view they take of almost all spiritualistic phenomena." He then argued that Myers' *Contemporary Review* article on automatic writing was unfair to the Spiritualist hypothesis of discarnate entities, and that the Myers-Gurney *Nineteenth Century* articles on apparitions stretched the telepathic concept much too far. Objecting to the whole line of reasoning thus far presented by practitioners of psychical research, "X." railed:

One naturally would conclude that the heads of a society for Psychical Research would believe in the Psyche; but if the telepathic theory is true, then the Society should be named the Society for Tele-Cerebral Research, or the Society for Occult Physiological Research.

It is well, I think, that we should all take it to heart that the Society, so far as it has proceeded, has not admitted any belief in mind, soul, or spirit apart from a human organisation; but has given us a telepathic theory which virtually says—mind, soul, spirit, are, so far as we know, only matter in motion. . . .

Mr. Myers expresses his opinion in his article in [*The*] *Contemporary* [*Review*], p. 243, that "the proceedings of the Society for Psychical Research must for a long time be largely occupied with telepathic researches." If so, I fear the subscribers to the Society may begin at last to feel that they do not get much for their money. . . .

But I have this against the managers of the Society, that, while inviting discussion at its public meetings, they most carefully withhold from their printed reports, the names and the thoughts of the few thinkers who venture to call the telepathic and other conclusions in question.[30]

This parting shot suggests that "X." was one of the Spiritualists on the S.P.R. council, perhaps even Stainton Moses. Rogers was certainly using *Light* to inform the Cambridge group that Spiritualist disaffection was growing, and probably to pressure them into rethinking their policy and perspective. He noted after the comments written by "X." that "letters frequently reach us regarding the attitude of the Society for Psychical Research to Spiritualism," while claiming innocently that "we insert the above in the interests of free discussion, and with no desire in the world to encourage any disparagement of the useful work which this Society is doing." But the message was clear, and the council heard it.

On March 14, 1885, *Light* featured a letter from S.P.R. council member Edward Pease that attempted to clear the air, at least on the Eglinton question. He explained that during the previous year he and other S.P.R. investigators had in fact held an unofficial series of sittings with Eglinton. These had not led to a full-scale investigation because the investigators had "obtained practically no phenomena of any sort."

In the March 21 issue, *Light* carried articles from both Gurney and Myers explaining the Cambridge group's point of view. Gurney's contribution to the debate included denials of the alleged materialism of the telepathic hypothesis and of any editorial censorship within the S.P.R. Myers followed with some typically Myersian words on the enormity of the issues. ("The question of communication with an invisible world is an enormously more important thing (for instance) than the etiology and treatment of typhoid-fever.") Then he went on to echo Sidgwick's view that resolving the question of nonmaterial mind was the sine qua non for any consideration of survival, whether from the Spiritualist or any other perspective. Counterattacking, he ventured the opinion that Spiritualists were deficient in their understanding of scientific thought, as well as in the delivery of quality evidence to the S.P.R. investigators. In closing, he painted a portrait of himself (and perhaps psychical research itself) as standing for a moderate middle way between the extremes of both Spiritualists and materialists. "When next I see myself described as 'a wild mystic, who must inevitably take the fatal plunge into the pit of Spiritualism, with all its stuffed hands, banjos, and nameless abominations,'" he wrote, "I shall try to console myself by the reflection that 'X.' considers me 'stranded in Agnosticism' and Mr. Haughton as an adept in the art of 'How not to do it.'"

Neither Rogers nor the Spiritualists were mollified, and the Eglinton question remained the focus for their general attack on S.P.R. attitudes toward Spiritualism. In the very next issue of *Light,* William Eglinton himself entered the controversy. He submitted that "Mr. Pease is by no means accurate in his letter, which appears in your last issue." The medium claimed he *had* produced effects for the S.P.R. investigators, although he admitted they were not of a particularly spectacular nature. In a commentary, Rogers said that while Eglinton had been comparatively subdued with Pease, the medium had performed adroitly with himself, C. C. Massey, Percy Wyndham, and other Spiritualist personnel of the Society.

In the May 16 *Light,* Haughton, the most militant Spiritualist spokesman, again challenged the S.P.R.'s entire handling of Spiritualism. This time he referred explicitly to the new organizational format whereby the council took no official responsibility for conclusions reached by investigating teams (even though it monitored the committees' work and screened their published output). The evasion of corporate endorsement of any single analysis was, to Sidgwick and the Cambridge group, a tactical device whereby the Society's scholarly reputation would not be risked on any given position.[31] But what was canny public relations to Sidgwick smacked of institutional cowardice and hypocrisy to the Spiritualists. Haughton added phenomena collected by a Spiritualist named Barkas to the range of evidence for Spiritualism ignored by the S.P.R. "To defer the inquiry [into the evidence collected by Barkas] till a more convenient season would only betray a desire to shirk it altogether," he sniffed. "And if the Society takes it up, I hope it will do so in a thorough-going manner, and pledge its own credit and honour for the result, be it what it may." Under Haughton's letter Rogers warned: "We again give place to correspondence of this nature because it is typical of communications which now constantly reach us."

In the September 19 issue of *Light,* Rogers publicized the fact that the S.P.R.'s approach to Spiritualism might be more offensive to Spiritualists than even Haughton had thought. The front page article in that issue consisted of "An Open Letter to Those Whom It May Concern" by John S. Farmer, the biographer of William Eglinton. Farmer had participated in one of the few séances that members of the S.P.R.'s physical phenomena committee had held, this time with a medium named Wendover. He announced to the readership of *Light* that one of the investigators had commented at the time that any participation by overt Spiritualists in S.P.R. studies of mediums raised the problem of controlling against complicity in fraud. Ruffled, Farmer had received a letter from that anonymous S.P.R. investigator. In it, the investigator had expressed regret that Farmer had been present at all at a particular séance. The investigator's position was that, for better or worse, the educated public seemed to consider most Spiritualists either accomplices in fraud or simple dupes. Farmer's presence, there-

fore, would inevitably be seen as "a weak point in the evidence."
Farmer was outraged. He argued that the incident "touches indirectly
on the whole attitude of the Society for Psychical Research towards
Spiritualism." He decried the whole S.P.R. orientation to the "outside
public, which you are so anxious to consider and convert" while the
Spiritualists, who were its real constituency, were "largely discounted
and passed by." In another reference to the body of Spiritualist opinion
supporting these objections, Farmer concluded: "I am afraid you will
regard my letter as being a grumble all around. At any rate, it is better
for any society to know what is being said of it."

Actually, Farmer and his fellow Spiritualists were making an
important point. From the beginning, the S.P.R. under Sidgwick had
indeed been far more oriented toward the outside public than toward
its own Spiritualist membership. The strategy Sidgwick pursued had
been the one that seemed most promising in ultimately persuading
that outside public of human survival of death. As an ethical
philosopher he was convinced of the necessity for publicly establishing
survival as a fact, or at least as a highly likely possibility. But he had
seen the establishment of nonmaterial mind as an absolutely crucial first
step in that direction: if the soul could be presented as a phenomenon
of this world, its projection into another after death might be more
meaningful a proposition to scientists and to the scientifically informed. Gurney and Myers were greatly interested in survival, but so
were many others. What distinguished Gurney and Myers were personal temperaments that meshed perfectly with Sidgwick's "this-
worldly" attack on the question of survival, personal temperaments
that were in fact ideally suited to Sidgwick's emphasis on nonmaterial
mind. It seems likely that it was they who dominated the Society's
output because Sidgwick's emphasis on mind corresponded to their
own peculiar visions of the inner life, and because they were the ones
with the most enthusiasm for psychical research as Sidgwick had de-
lineated it. They were the ones most willing to commit practically
their entire lives to it.

Gurney and Myers' forays into thought transference, mesmerism, and the like had yielded in the telepathic hypothesis an analysis of mind that essentially confirmed their own personal belief in the limitless horizons of inner experience. But the result, as the Spiritualists realized, was output with which no real Spiritualist could feel comfortable. They must have expected psychical research to hold the question of survival in abeyance, at least temporarily. But they could hardly have expected an interpretive framework that at best ignored their own hypothesis of disembodied entities, and at worst eclipsed it. That is precisely what they got in telepathic mind, as could be seen from Myers' paper on automatic writing and, perhaps more ominously, in Myers and Gurney's formulations on apparitions. While the psychical researchers had thus far confined their study to apparitions of the near-dead and not the dead, Spiritualists could hardly fail to feel alarmed at this progressive extension of the range of phenomena psychical research interpreted as telepathic manifestations.

The telepathic mind, however wondrous, was (as, indeed, its discoverers had intended it to be) entirely a fact of this world, our organisms, earthly life. But the Spiritualists, for all their empiricism, had always held an essentially traditional view of the spirit and the soul. To them, the soul was more than a fact of our organisms and earthly life. The soul was "the soul" precisely because it survived death to exist in some dimension beyond earthly life. Authentication of that survival authenticated the soul for the Spiritualists, and nothing else. But in the *Proceedings* and the articles in outside journals, psychical research was being deliberately identified in the public mind as an inquiry into the potentialities of the human mechanism in this world rather than as a confirmation of its projection into another after death. Psychical researchers didn't seem to have the same orientation toward the soul as Spiritualists did at all. Not surprisingly, the minutes of council meetings show members' resignations accelerating markedly throughout 1885.

Light began the year 1886 with an exchange between Rogers and Barrett. Ironically, Barrett had never enjoyed cordial relations with the Sidgwick group. He had always been somewhat closer to the Spiritualists, which may be why Rogers was so stung by a lecture Barrett gave in Norwich at which he was reported to have said that "muscular motion accounts for nine-tenths of the so-called Spiritualism." In the January 13 issue of *Light,* Rogers called Barrett to task for the remark, complaining that "this gratuitous slur on 'the so-called Spiritualism' was incomprehensible" unless "it be a fact, as many Spiritualists have come to believe, that this is but a part of the role which some of the leading members of the Society for Psychical Research have decided to play."

On January 16, Barrett tried to offer a measured response to *Light* readers. He denied using the term "so-called Spiritualism," then vaguely noted that "Spiritualism belongs not to the Spiritual but to the phenomenal order of things and as such comes within the scope of scientific inquiry." Any interpretation attendant on such an inquiry, he advised, "may then be different from that usually entertained by Spiritualists." But on January 23 Rogers retorted in *Light* that Barrett's reply was unsatisfactory to him and to "the many Spiritualists who, rightly or wrongly, suspect that some of the leading members of the Society for Psychical Research are in the habit of speaking of Spiritualism in terms of depreciation and disparagement."

Barrett took a step backward on January 30, agreeing that while "exact scientific inquiry demands the most laborious processes," Spiritualists in fact had a legitimate grievance in that some public presentation of the evidence for the physical phenomena of Spiritualism was due from the S.P.R. On the other hand, Frederic Myers did not feel the S.P.R. owed anything to anyone. Insisting in the same issue that his own attitude toward Spiritualism was one of "cautious hesitancy and not of deliberate hostility," he chided Spiritualists for their intolerance of the analytical method and repeated his charge that they had not been generous with data from private circles (as opposed to professional mediumistic displays). But both Barrett's and Myers' comments were buried in the correspondence section of the issue. The unsigned lead article of that issue of *Light* actually announced that no data from private circles would be forthcoming unless the architects of the S.P.R.'s policy toward Spiritualism "have purged themselves by a frank avowal of mistakes made, or by a withdrawal of the offensive imputations against Spiritualists; or, on the other hand, until the Society disclaims the actions of their lieutenants."

It was in June 1886 that the final showdown began. In the S.P.R. *Journal* that month, Mrs. Sidgwick discussed reports sent in by members on séances held with Eglinton. She was at the time chairwoman of the physical phenomena committee, and had visited Eglinton herself in that capacity (bending her husband's guidelines in deference to the Spiritualist demand). Eglinton had not impressed her, nor had all the testimony sent to the *Journal* by Spiritualist members of the S.P.R. She expressed in her own *Journal* article "no hesitation in attributing [Eglinton's] performance to clever conjuring." The witnesses, she said, had greatly overestimated their own powers of observation, particularly their ability to concentrate attention without distraction. In addition, a report by Hodgson in the same edition of the *Journal* emphasized that a constant stream of distractions occurred in every Eglinton séance. Essentially, every Spiritualist who had publicly endorsed Eglinton in the *Journal* had just been called a dupe.

The outcry was enormous, and subsequent issues of the S.P.R. *Journal* were deluged with attacks on the skeptics. In the June 5 edition of *Light,* the Spiritualist C. C. Massey (an S.P.R. investigator who had remained loyal to the Society throughout, despite his own misgivings) tried desperately to intervene. Reminding Spiritualists that the Society held no corporate opinions, he announced that both he and Barrett disagreed with Mrs. Sidgwick. He was in fact preparing a paper attacking her that would be read at the next general meeting. But for many Spiritualists, Massey's initiative already seemed too little and too late. On June 12, G. D. Haughton wrote a letter to *Light* expressing the Spiritualist state of mind regarding the Society for Psychical Research in general and its disclaimer of any official or corporately sanctioned positions in particular.

"C.C.M." is certainly the finest example I know of that Christian charity which "hopeth all things, believeth all things, endureth all things." His patience and hope are quite inexhaustible. But surely his all-condoning amiability impairs the clearness of his vision, and makes him blind to obvious facts? He is not "aware that even the doubts of individual members, however honoured or distinguished, have any claim to be accepted as *characteristic of the Society.*" What! not when two members in especial—to wit, Messrs. Myers and Gurney, and one or two more in a lesser degree—have been selected by the Society to conduct their investigations; have been allowed to monopolise the platform at the meetings of the Society, almost to the exclusion of everybody else; have been permitted to have the lion's share in the printed *Proceedings* of the Society, and to ventilate their theories as often as they please, and without stint of space; in short, to appropriate to themselves well-nigh the whole visible arena of the Society. . . . We must be thankful for small mercies, and I congratulate "C.C.M." on his being graciously permitted to review "Mrs. Sidgwick's judgement." But I trust that he will express himself on this unlooked for occasion with modesty and discretion, and not blurt out any rude opinions which might try too far the forebearance of the Society.[32]

Not surprisingly, the Society's next general meeting, as reported in the July 10 *Light,* was the most dramatic one held so far. Massey argued that the real issue raised by Mrs. Sidgwick was the acceptability of any human testimony on Spiritualist phenomena. By her standards, no human testimony in that area would ever be allowed. Spiritualists had to disagree with such a position. "This is a plain issue," Massey declared, "and one on which it behooves us to have a clear opinion. For, if Mrs. Sidgwick's view is adopted in this Society, we may at once renounce that part of our original programme which referred to the objective phenomena of Spiritualism, it being extremely unlikely that sufficient material for judgment will be offered . . . from evidence independent of the senses and minds of witnesses." In the subsequent discussion, Stainton Moses thanked Massey on behalf of all Spiritualists for "one of the best reasoned arguments in defence of their faith he had ever heard." Then Moses, who had been leery of the entire enterprise of psychical research from the beginning, presented the condition for continued Spiritualist support of the Society: corporate disavowal of Mrs. Sidgwick's position, expressed from the chair. After other Spiritualists were heard from, Myers reiterated the Society's usual "no corporate opinions" position and suggested that if Spiritualists were unhappy they had the alternative of electing more appropriate council members. Turning to Stainton Moses, Myers publicly reminded the celebrated medium that he had never supplied the Society with the sort of private data it had been requesting for years.

The Spiritualists, however, would have no more of either the Society's standards of evidence or of its defense of interpretive pluralism. The latter in particular was meaningless. It was the public image of psychical research that mattered. The Spiritualists had always been the closest monitors of the S.P.R.'s presentation of psychical research to the public because they had expected from that presentation a wider scientific and popular endorsement of Spiritualism. What they had gotten instead was greater public awareness of views either irrelevant or overtly hostile to Spiritualism, and as long as the Cambridge group ran the Society that would continue to be the case. Mrs. Sidgwick's article was only one, if the single most offensive, example of the S.P.R.'s publicly promulgated orientation. A reversal was necessary, and promptly.

The Society was at a turning point. The July 10 edition of *Light* had announced ominously that "unless an official disavowal of Mrs. Sidgwick's article, as being representative of the views of the Society, is forthwith made, the duty of all Spiritualists, who are members of the Society for Psychical Research, will be obvious." As Stainton Moses, "M.A. (Oxon.)," made clear in his front-page article in *Light*'s July 24 edition, a mass Spiritualist defection was impending. He warned of "a schism in the Society which would, not improbably, split it to the core." The options could not have been made clearer to the S.P.R.'s leaders.

The corporate disavowal of Mrs. Sidgwick's position was never made. Resignations recorded in the minutes of the council meetings reveal that the threatened Spiritualist desertion in fact took place throughout the rest of 1886. The turnover of members was voluminous. As Massey, Moses, and Rogers resigned, the Spiritualist presence in the S.P.R. council was reduced to a minimum.

But the minutes of those same council meetings also record that the Spiritualists were replaced by new subscribers, and that the Society lost very little in terms of overall membership figures. For when Spiritualists and Spiritualism were screened (or forced) out, the S.P.R. and psychical research were left with something uniquely their own. The complexities and capacities of the human personality would now clearly constitute the field, and a highly distinctive vision of them would be more vividly articulated over the next decade and a half.

With it, psychical research would attract its own public.

Notes

1. R. Laurence Moore's book contains a fine treatment of psychical research in America. Aside from that, however, the only professional historians who have investigated the subject are the historians of science Seymour Mauskopf and Michael McVaugh. Their work focuses on the issue of how psychical research of the 1930s (when it came to be known as "parapsychology") was related by its practitioners to accepted scientific paradigms of the time, and the response of the scientific community to it ("J. B. Rhine's 'Extra-Sensory Perception' and Its Background in Psychical Research," *Isis,* vol. 67 [June 1976], pp. 161–89).

Most accounts of the history of psychical research have been written by psychical researchers themselves. Among the more informative are: Hereward Carrington's *The Story of Psychic Science* (New York: Ives Washburn, 1931); Charles Richet's *Thirty Years of Psychical Research* (New York: Macmillan, 1923); and D. Scott Rogo's *Parapsychology: A Century of Inquiry* (New York: Taplinger, 1975). Gardner Murphy's *The Challenge of Psychical Research* (New York: Harper and Row, 1961) also contains historical material.

The best of these "in-house" histories is certainly Alan Gauld's *The Founders of Psychical Research.* Gauld, a psychologist, is a practicing psychical researcher. His focus, as might be expected, is on the objective truth of some of the phenomena Spiritualism and the Society for Psychical Research have brought to light.

2. Horatio Donkin, "On Thought-Reading," *The Nineteenth Century,* vol. 12 (July-December 1882), p. 132.

3. *Proceedings,* vol. 1, p. 8.

4. Ibid., p. 12.

5. Of course, it would always be argued by opponents of psychical research that what was really required to demonstrate the reality of the phenomena they investigated and the existence of nonmaterial mind in general was not testimony in volume but rather *replicable* experiments. C. E. M. Hansel's *ESP: A Scientific Evaluation* (New York: Scribner's, 1966) is a fairly recent indictment of the entire field of psychical research or parapsychology on the grounds that its practitioners never understood the nature of scientific evidence. Psychical researchers were aware of that argument from the beginning. Their response was that to assume the phenomena they investigated *were* replicable implied the wholly unwarranted assumption that they conformed to known natural law. For that reason they felt their own standards of evidence to be the only appropriate ones, at least during the inquiry's early stages. Edmund Gurney expressed that position in "On the Nature of Evidence in Matters Extraordinary," *National Review,* vol. 4 (1884) pp. 472–91. Opponents could and did retort that if the phenomena investigated did not conform to *some* natural law, they either did not really occur or were outside the purview of science until such time as natural law itself was recast to account for them. Horatio Donkin in particular would continue criticizing psychical research on the grounds that true science proceeded from the known to the unknown, while psychical research did the opposite ("Mystery-Mongering," *The Saturday Review of Politics, Literature, Science and Art,* vol. 56 [August 4, 1883], pp. 595–96).

The reader is left to determine the merits of each point of view for himself. The scientific truth of psychical research's findings is quite outside the scope of this study, which is concerned with the image of human selfhood offered by the psychical researchers and people's belief in it.

6. *Proceedings,* vol. 1, p. 12.

7. Ibid., p. 11.

8. Ibid.

9. Ibid., p. 34.

10. Sidgwick was referring specifically to an article in the *Pall Mall Gazette* of October 21, 1882, which stated that "the scientific attitude can only be maintained by careful abstention from dangerous trains of thought."

11. *Proceedings,* vol. 1, pp. 70–97.

12. Ibid., p. 147.

13. Ibid., pp. 251–63; vol. 2 (1884), pp. 12–20, 61–73.

14. James Braid, *Magic, Witchcraft, Animal Magnetism, Hypnotism, and Electro-Biology* (Edinburgh: A. and C. Black, 1852).

15. Rudolf Heidenhain, *Hypnotism or Animal Magnetism* (London, 1888; reprint of German edition, 1880), p. 5.

16. Jean-Martin Charcot, *Clinical Lectures*, 3 vols. (London, 1887).

17. A. A. Liébeault, *Etude sur le zoomagnétisme* (Paris, 1883).

18. *Proceedings*, vol. 1, pp. 252–62.

19. The thought transference results obtained in the Creery and Smith-Blackburn investigations were supplemented primarily by experiments initiated independently by Malcolm Guthrie, J. P., in Liverpool (ibid., pp. 263–83). Gurney and Myers continued Guthrie's work there. It was those experiments that brought the Nobel-Prize-winning physicist, Sir Oliver Lodge, into the S.P.R.

20. By this time, the *Proceedings*, which were assembled by a separate publications committee within the council, were consciously distributed in the most efficacious manner possible. On April 24, 1883, it was decided to send the first collected set of them to leading London newspapers for review. On June 8, two thousand copies of the second set were sent to the United States and the British colonies, free of charge. On July 17, a second edition of the second set was sent to "Scientific Societies, Scientific Journals at home and abroad, and as far as is found practicable to Free Libraries, Mechanics' Institutes, and Literary Institutions" (Minutes, Council meeting).

21. *Proceedings*, vol. 2, pp. 109–36; *The Nineteenth Century*, vol. 15 (May 1884), pp. 791–815.

22. "A Theory of Apparitions, Part II" reveals their confidence. It was read to the Society on May 28, 1884 (*Proceedings*, vol. 2, pp. 157–86) and published in *The Nineteenth Century* that June.

23. Theosophy was an attempted synthesis of Western rationalism and Eastern mysticism leavened by Madame Blavatsky's personal mediumship. It was a subject of great interest to Spiritualists, as even a cursory glance through the pages of *Light* or any other Spiritualist publication indicates. Hodgson's report, published in the *Proceedings* in 1885, charged that Theosophy and Madame Blavatsky were entirely fraudulent.

24. *Light*, February 3, 1883, p. 54.

25. *Proceedings*, vol. 1, p. 246.

26. Council meeting of February 5, 1884, Minute 12. Council meeting of October 16, 1884, Minute 7.

27. This was the point at which an honorary secretary was created to handle the content of S.P.R. publications, and Gurney was given the office. Minute 12 of the council meeting of December 30, 1884, records that the

president "thought this change on the whole desirable, especially in those areas of inquiry which had hitherto engaged the Society's attention; and he thought it still more important in regard to other branches which were likely to engage the attention of the Society in the future, and in the investigation of which it was probable that there would be greater difference of individual opinion than in those matters which had mainly occupied them in the past." Sidgwick's first three-year tenure as president was almost up, and he achieved passage of this resolution just before handing the office over, temporarily, to Balfour Stewart on February 13, 1885.

28. F. W. H. Myers, "Automatic Writing, or the Rationale of Planchette," *The Contemporary Review,* vol. 47 (1885), p. 249.

29. *Light,* March 7, 1885, pp. 112–13.

30. *Light,* March 14, 1885, p. 121.

31. Sidgwick, discussing plans for a book on apparitions *(Phantasms of the Living),* had written: "I have come to the conclusion that all our appearances in print ought to be conducted on the principle of individual responsibility. In this obscure and treacherous region, girt about with foes watching eagerly for some bad blunder, it is needlessly increasing our risks to run the danger of *two* reputations being exploded by one blunder. . . . Let the responsibility *before the world* be always attached to *one,* that we may sell our reputations as dearly as possible" (quoted from Alan Gauld, *The Founders of Psychical Research,* p. 161). Sidgwick was referring specifically to the idea of having Gurney write the bulk of *Phantasms of the Living,* but notification of the fact that membership in the S.P.R. did not identify anyone with any given view appeared on every publication the Society ever issued, and still does.

32. *Light,* June 12, 1886, p. 269.

Chapter Five

From Noumenal Selfhood
to Subliminal Consciousness:
The S.P.R., 1886–1900

THE AVANT-GARDE

In Europe the debate on hypnosis to which Gurney had originally related his own work on mesmerism was accelerating. At Le Havre experiments had been conducted that tended to support the Nancy school against the Salpêtrière in its contention that not all phenomena of hypnotism were reducible to phsyiological operations. Pierre Janet, while still a student in Charcot's own Société de Psychologie Physiologique, had reported as early as 1885 on the experiments conducted by a Dr. J. H. A. Gilbert at Le Havre that seemed to reinforce the contention that there was more to hypnotism than a physiologically generated abnormality. By 1888, Salpêtrière representatives Alfred Binet and Charles Féré had mounted a full-scale counterattack in the form of a book entitled, derisively, *Le Magnetisme Animal.*

Myers had spent some time at Le Havre with Janet and other Continental investigators. In fact, in 1885 he had drawn on those and the Nancy school's experiments to write a paper suggesting that hypnotism might open a channel into that "non-physiological compartment of mind where moral codes resided." In his view, the possibility existed that human personality was perfectible through hypnotic suggestion.[1] Myers was willing to propose such speculations because psychical research was on the threshold of its next conceptual leap forward.

At the time, Myers and Gurney were attempting to mesh the

findings of anti-Salpêtrière investigators of hypnosis with their own concept of telepathy. Actually, the Continental work on hypnosis was infusing the psychical researchers with a new vigor. Paranormal phenomena such as thought transference, wherein mind operated independently on mind, had in their opinion revealed a whole stratum of mental activity that transcended the constraints of matter. If phenomena of the hypnotic trance also represented the telepathic force at work, and in peculiarly intense form, then studies of the human personality in the trance state might provide clues to the source of telepathy itself. Gurney and Myers were theorizing that telepathic mental activity might be to the trance-state personality what a religious service was to a cathedral: a form of activity simultaneously contained within and projecting from an overarching, structural framework. They thought that overarching framework might actually be an entirely distinct level or form of human personality. Far from relating telepathy to the idea of surviving death, they were actually plunging even deeper into the organization of human selfhood. Myers had expressly interpreted certain hypnotic phenomena as expressions of the telepathic mental realm as early as 1886. On the basis of Le Havre experiments observed with Janet and others, he argued that hypnotism represented at least in part a telepathic phenomenon. Whereas Charcot had seen it as a means of understanding the physiology of hysteria, Myers argued that it pointed to something far vaster. "Hypnotism," he concluded, "writes for us the secret of the psychical mechanism of man."[2]

It was Gurney, however, who really blazed the path. He was quite conversant with developments on the Continent (the S.P.R. council had voted to fund a trip to France). But he also continued working with his own protégé, G. A. Smith. The latter continued to astonish. What most impressed Gurney was Smith's posthypnotic performance of commands and memory of hallucinations that had been imparted when he was entranced, and of which he seemed to possess no conscious recall. Gurney was fascinated by this indication that the entranced mind was capable of preserving its own memories and in-

stigating behavior of its own, independent of input derived from the
normal state of consciousness. To him, this implied that the trance
state might actually constitute neither a temporary loss of normal
consciousness nor a hyperacute phase of it but rather an altogether
distinct, secondary level of consciousness itself. That is, the trance state
might be the portal through which one passed into a telepathic realm of
being, an entirely different form of selfhood.

Gurney felt himself to be on the threshold of discovering
scientifically a whole new level of existence. His dream of verifying the
reality of "inner man," of making phenomenological the metaphysical,
seemed to be approaching realization. Nor was he at all timorous about
what he might find in that submerged stratum. Indeed, his goal was to
set it free.

> Hypnotism assumes a wholly new significance when it leads . . . to
> results *beyond itself*—when it appears as the ready means for establishing
> a secondary train of consciousness. . . . And it would be a yet further
> development if in a particular hypnotic phenomenon, such as induced
> hallucination, we found the means for straining such secondary con-
> sciousness free from any association with the ostensible "self," and assur-
> ing to it a perfectly independent flow. . . . In the new psychology, the
> line between the normal and abnormal has become so shadowy that not
> the smallest abnormal phenomenon can be safely neglected by those
> who aim at the fullest possible realisation of human nature and
> development.[3]

If Gurney was unafraid to open the door to the secondary stratum,
Myers was unabashedly anxious to rush through it. He demonstrated
that in an article he wrote for *The Nineteenth Century* in November
1886. In that paper, entitled "Multiplex Personality," Myers presented
to the outside world the perspective from which psychical researchers
were appraising the new territory opened up by investigations into
hypnotism. He actually argued that the secondary level (or levels) of
consciousness suggested by certain hypnotic phenomena could be
viewed in terms of the evolutionary process. His rumination began
with a catalogue of the benefits already derived from hypnotic sugges-

tion when practiced therapeutically (alleviation of pain, anxiety, fatigue). Then it went on to suggest that the level of being evoked in trance induction, radically different and in a sense superior to that known in everyday consciousness, might provide the form of life that future generations would know. As our forebears had shed their fur, so might we eventually shed the form of consciousness presently experienced in favor of something better.

> And surely, here, as in Galahad's cry of "If I lose myself, I find myself," we have a hint that much, very much, of what we are wont to regard as an integral part of us may drop away, and yet leave us with a consciousness of our being which is more vivid and purer than before. This web of habits and appetites, of lusts and fears, is not, perhaps, the ultimate manifestation of what in truth we are. It is the cloak which our rude forefathers have woven themselves against the cosmic storm; but we are already learning to shift and refashion it as our gentler weather needs; and if perchance it slip from us in the sunshine then something more ancient and more glorious is for a moment guessed within.[4]

When he referred rhapsodically to that other level of consciousness, "more glorious" than "this web of habits and appetites, of lusts and fears," Myers was probably alluding to his own ideal of the inner life. But at the time he lacked the tools to describe or express that vision adequately. Considerations of the "secondary self" and the "multiplex personality" were in 1886 still the outer fringe, the *avant-garde* of psychical research. Mainstream work still revolved around the concept of telepathy, on which Myers and Gurney's further musings on alternative forms of selfhood were based. In October of that year, the Society for Psychical Research presented its most ambitious formulation of that concept.

THE MAINSTREAM: CRISIS AND REORIENTATION

The massive, two-volume *Phantasms of the Living* was the result of the S.P.R.'s long inquiry into visual hallucinations and crisis apparitions.

Authorship was attributed jointly to Gurney, Myers, and Frank Podmore, but in fact Myers wrote only the introduction, and Podmore had only investigated some of the cases. The bulk of the book was really Edmund Gurney's.[5]

Phantasms was the first real magnum opus of psychical research. The work was an organization of, and commentary on, 702 cases of a particular form of hallucination collected by Gurney and the literary committee. The core of its argument related to crisis apparitions (defined as the hallucination of a particular individual within twelve hours, either way, of his death). Gurney and the literary committee had for the preceding several years conducted a survey to achieve some estimate of the percentage of the total population that had experienced hallucinations in general and crisis apparitions in particular. The per diem national death rate at the time was one in every 16,500, which to the psychical researchers meant that an individual experiencing any hallucination of another individual should have a 1 in 16,500 chance probability of hallucinating an image of a dying person. But Gurney argued that the ratio of reported cases of crisis apparitions to the total population exposed to the S.P.R. appeal yielded a figure far in excess of that expected on the basis of randomness.[6] Concluding that another variable must be present, he proceeded to make the case for telepathy. In the S.P.R. style, the 702 cases were categorized in terms of the quality of evidence for telepathy each offered. Finally, after this statistical case for crisis apparitions as telepathic phenomena, the work concluded with a general argument for the existence of telepathy as evidenced by the transfer of mental images in a variety of ways.

Phantasms of the Living was an important work in the internal evolution of psychical research. It went beyond apparitions of the near-dead to include those of the recently dead under the heading of telepathic phenomena. In that way, it furthered the distance between Spiritualists' and psychical researchers' understandings of what really might be happening when one's senses (in this case, one's eyes) indicated that the observer was in the presence of a revenant. The work was even more significant, however, as a representation of psychical research to the public. *Phantasms of the Living* was published by the Society for Psychical Research itself. It was the first representation of the discipline to which the S.P.R. committed its own name. If there was to be a public image of what psychical research was, Gurney's work explicitly showed that the idea of the telepathic mind was its basis.

But while Spiritualists had found the concept of telepathy in a sense too conservative, elements of the scientific world considered it wildly extravagant. When *Phantasms of the Living* was first published, it drew little attention. A year later, however, serious attacks appeared. The August 1887 edition of *The Nineteenth Century* contained an article by A. T. Innes charging that the heart of the matter was verification of the fact that Gurney's percipients had really experienced what they said they did. Demonstration of that, Innes claimed, required letters or statements of some sort made out at the actual time of the experience. He argued that this would have been the logical thing for percipients to have done, yet Gurney had uncovered no such documents. Another criticism of Gurney's work appeared in, of all places, the December 1887 *Proceedings* of the American S.P.R. That organization (generally somewhat more Spiritualistically inclined than its British counterpart) gave its pages over to an article by the American philosopher C. S. Peirce, who accused Gurney of several major errors. Peirce claimed that each of the 702 cases Gurney had compiled violated important standards of evidence. He also charged that, statistically, Gurney's computation of randomness in the likelihood of experiencing a crisis apparition was misconceived.

The reception accorded *Phantasms of the Living* was a serious reversal for the entire discipline. Gurney, however, faced the challenges forthrightly. He replied to Innes in the following issue of *The Nineteenth Century,* stating that it was not at all likely that percipients would have either made or preserved depositions of their experience and that the mass of data collected was not vitiated by that omission. Turning to Peirce, he argued that the American had misrepresented every single case he had discussed. In fact, exchanges with critics of *Phantasms of the Living* were what primarily occupied the rest of Gurney's brief life.

On June 23, 1888, he was discovered dead in a hotel room in Brighton. The cause of death was ascertained as an accidental overdose of chloroform, after Alfred Gurney testified that his brother had often used narcotics to relieve neuralgia and insomnia.[7] Gurney's death was another major setback for the S.P.R. Then, before the shock had really worn off, disaster struck again.

In 1888, follow-up experiments on the Creery children revealed their use of a code. The children had provided an important part of the original arsenal of data on thought transference, which in turn had led to the entire concept of the telepathic mind. With the Creery material now suspect, the very foundations of mainstream psychical research were imperiled. This was a critical juncture for the S.P.R. Intelligent decisions had to be made, and quickly.

William Barrett, who considered himself entitled to recognition as the discoverer of thought transference, insisted that the earlier Creery findings were not affected by recent chicanery. But the Sidgwick group opted for a less complacent course. They decided to excise all Creery experiments from the case for telepathy. That tottering notion would be reinforced with brand-new data, data that would rebuild the tele- pathic argument in general while parrying critics of *Phantasms of the Living* in particular.

Officially, the S.P.R. embarked upon a new project: the Census of Hallucinations, which was cast along the same lines as Gurney's work. It too was a statistical reckoning of the chance likelihood of individuals receiving visual images of others who were physically out of sight, as opposed to the actual numerical incidence of them. However, it was on a far larger scale than anything Gurney had done. Gurney had received some five thousand responses to his questionnaire. The Census of Hallucinations would process over seventeen thousand. In 1889 Mrs. Sidgwick would assume command of the new committee formed to conduct the Census, and output from that committee would be as prominently featured in the Society's *Proceedings* as the thought transfer- ence and literary committees' work had been previously.[8]

Mainstream psychical research had been shaken but not shattered. The S.P.R. was regrouping. In fact, it was about to enter what might be considered its most adventurous period. The entire discipline was about to be reinvigorated by events in the United States.

Mrs. Leonora Piper, the wife of a Boston store clerk, is probably the most important figure in the history of psychical research outside of active investigators themselves. She was a medium in a sense, but of a very special kind. Her mediumship, never commercially exploited and therefore not dismissable under Sidgwick's guidelines, would stretch the discipline's, and particularly Myers', understanding of human personality in the most profound way. Mrs. Piper's association with psychical research began shortly after a visit to a blind healing medium for assistance with a tumor. Soon thereafter, Mrs. Piper began unaccountably drifting off into spontaneous trances. In that condition, she never once attempted to display any prowess in spectacular physical phenomena, *à la* D. D. Home. However, she did reveal startlingly accurate facts to those present, facts that were allegedly revealed to her by a spirit control. Her purely "mental" mediumship created a sizable stir.[9]

William James, who would become the most noteworthy figure in American psychical research, learned of Mrs. Piper through his mother-in-law. While doubtful that she was informed by any spirit control, he became convinced by his sittings with her that she did indeed possess supernormal mental powers of some sort. Further investigation into this case, he decided, was vital.

James himself, of course, had numerous other commitments. The American Society for Psychical Research, which might plausibly have been expected to conduct an inquiry into the Piper case, had no Cambridge group to drive and subsidize it. So, in response to James' reports, the British S.P.R. sent Richard Hodgson both to investigate Mrs. Piper and to "reorganize" the American Society. Hodgson would remain for fifteen years. The extended Piper inquiry he initiated would constitute perhaps the single most important research undertaking in the history of psychical research. Mrs. Piper was brought to England several times. Reports of experimentation with her, along with the census of hallucinations, dominated the published output of the S.P.R. into the early 1890s.

The complexity of the Piper case derived in large part from the baffling nature of her alleged spirit controls. The first of these, "Phinuit," claimed to be a French doctor. However, he knew little of either medicine or the French language, and was capable of the most obvious deceptions. This seemed to discredit the notion that he was the spirit he claimed to be. At the same time, he was capable of what the psychical researchers considered truly remarkable feats of knowledge acquisition. They could interpret what appeared to be his supernormal mental capacities as telepathic phenomena, but they were left with the problem of accounting for why or how what had to be an aspect of Mrs. Piper's own mind was working through or with some completely alternate character. The second of Mrs. Piper's controls, "George Pelham," was even more radically divergent in nature from the normal Leonora Piper than Phinuit had been, and also seemed even more telepathically adroit. If the controls were not spirits, they nonetheless seemed to be something quite alien to Leonora Piper herself. The questions were: who or what were they, and where did they come from? Hodgson actually had Mrs. Piper trailed by private detectives to learn whether or not she was consciously acquiring the information her controls gave out, but this sleuthing was to no avail.

At the time, Myers was trying to reshape the interpretive overview of the entire discipline in the manner he and Gurney had already plotted. The Piper case fascinated him because it seemed to indicate further that the telepathic mind should be understood as a property of what was actually a submerged stratum (or even strata) of the human personality. On the basis of the Piper case and other material, Myers was in fact trying to reorient mainstream psychical research by fitting telepathy itself into an even larger conceptual framework. He believed that by taking this direction psychical research could perhaps recast or even replace the subspecialty of "abnormal psychology," or the study of atypical mental phenomena. At the time, that did not seem an impossible ambition.

The S.P.R. and the International Congresses of Experimental Psychology

Between Gurney's death and the turn of the century, the most characteristic (and probably the most carefully chosen) representations of psychical research as a discipline came in the form of S.P.R. contributions to the International Congresses of Experimental Psychology. Those multinational assemblies were in effect attempts by elements of the new profession of psychology (whose practitioners were still recruited from places like the School of Moral Sciences at Cambridge) to establish its identity. The crucial debate running through the first several congresses was the relationship of psychology to physiology, anatomy, and medicine.

The work of the S.P.R. was prominently featured at the first congress, which was held in Paris in 1889 and attended by some two hundred psychologists. Not surprisingly, the Society representatives' presentation of their discipline lent support to the school favoring a concept of mind not exclusively contingent on brain matter. Actually, the nonphysiological school was generally in the ascendant in that congress. Charcot, who had convened the assembly, was indisposed. In his absence, the first official motion enacted was the replacement of his title for the gathering, the Congress of Physiological Psychology, with a new one, the Congress for Experimental Psychology. The implicit rebuff to the physiological school was reinforced when Secretary Charles Richet, a professor of physiology who would become the most illustrious representative of psychical research in France, argued that the statistical study of hallucinations undertaken by the S.P.R. in Britain and America should be supplemented by similar work on the Continent. The question of hallucinations was one of four main topics discussed at the congress. Others were heredity, muscular sense, and hypnotism. In the meetings on hypnotism, Myers and Sidgwick were cautious. They advanced only the position that subtle clues and suggestions assimilated by the senses did not account for all the phenomena of the hypnotic trance, that there was indeed a manifestation of the telepathic property in the trance state.[10]

The S.P.R. representatives knew that subsequent congresses would rouse the ire of psychologists whose idea of mental life was not reinforced at the Paris conclave. The Germans, in particular, were disaffected. They spoke derisively of "suprascientific tendencies of the left borderland."[11] But that "left borderland" was by then both numerous and convinced that there was more to mind than matter—and so the international congresses continued to be held. The next was scheduled for London in 1892. Professor Wundt gloomily predicted in his *Philosophische Studien* that as hypnotism ("the romance of psychology") had been the dominant topic in Paris, so would telepathy ("the climax of romance") keynote the discussions in London. He was quite right.[12] The confidence of the psychical researchers was growing apace with that of an entire wing of the psychological profession.

Sidgwick, in fact, was the London congress's presiding officer.[13] The S.P.R.'s contribution represented a further elaboration of what psychical research meant, and particularly the interpretive canopy it was trying to construct. A report of the census of hallucinations and a paper by Mrs. Sidgwick on the accumulated evidence for thought transference affirmed the concept of telepathy.[14] And Myers presented the new conceptual overview of psychical research with papers on the "Experimental Induction of Hallucination"[15] and "Crystal Vision." Particularly in the latter, he argued that the telepathic property of mental life actually reflected the existence of an entire, hidden stratum of personality. "Crystal Vision" was about "anterograde amnesia," a term coined by Charcot to describe the condition of people who cannot retain new memories. Janet had submitted that some such people in fact did reveal those memories in hypnotic and dream states. Myers supplemented Janet's findings by arguing that such dormant memories could also be revived in some people by prolonged staring at flat, bright surfaces. To him, this suggested that those memories must exist in some subconscious dimension. It was already known that sensory processes were sometimes insufficient to imprint a recent event on normal, waking consciousness, but research on anterograde amnesia indicated to Myers that some trans-sensory operation might be feeding and enlarging a secondary level of consciousness, evoked by crystal gazing.

Myers was groping toward something. He couldn't yet clarify what the subconscious or the secondary self was, but the Piper material was making an increasingly strong case, in his opinion, that it existed. In the 1896 Congress of Experimental Psychology, held in Munich, he presented a lengthy paper on events observed by himself and others in Mrs. Piper's trance states ("A Record of Observation of Certain Phenomena of Trance").[16] It was preceded by the Sidgwicks' defense of the census of hallucinations and the idea of telepathy against criticism from Germany and Denmark.[17] Coming as it did on the heels of those papers, Myers' remarks on Mrs. Piper strengthened the notion that psychical research, while still in the process of conclusively verifying the telepathic mode of mental activity, was already linking that range of phenomena to an entire stratum of being lying below the level of normal, daily existence. Myers and the other S.P.R. investigators of Mrs. Piper (including Hodgson, Oliver Lodge, and Walter Leaf) were still tentative in their conclusions. But they were inclining to the view that the utterances and actions of Mrs. Piper's spirit controls were manifestations of some stratum of her selfhood whose characteristics were foreign to those of the normal, waking Leonora Piper.

The S.P.R. had come a long way from the Sidgwick group's original inquiries into Spiritualism. The Society's representation of its work at the International Congresses of Experimental Psychology helped demonstrate this. To anyone who was listening, psychical research was a foray into the actual nature and composition of human selfhood in this world. In fact, it was on the verge of offering the psychological profession as comprehensive an interpretation of personal identity as had yet been heard. Actually, a fair number of psychologists were listening rather closely. Many would find cause for hope in psychical research.

THE SECULAR SOUL

From about 1892 onwards, the *Proceedings* of the S.P.R. featured a number of articles by Myers in which he set forth his concept of the "subliminal self." These were Myers' final and most significant contributions to the field of psychical research. He died in 1901. Prior to his death, however, he compiled major portions of those articles into a large, unfinished book entitled *Human Personality and Its Survival of Bodily Death.* The work was published posthumously in 1903.[18] It constitutes, for all its incompleteness and confused, sometimes barely readable prose, the best expression of what psychical research meant by the turn of the century.[19]

That can be said because Myers made a deliberate attempt to synthesize the entire corpus of psychical research until that time. Each stage in the development of his ideas is presented as the end point of a consideration of a wide range of phenomena with which the S.P.R. had been dealing for a generation. Apparitions, for example, are treated only after Myers has surveyed the entire literature collected by the Society on the telepathic conveyance of images, dreams, hallucinations, crystal vision, and other subjects. The analysis he ultimately draws from apparitions, hypnotic phenomena, and a host of other subjects (especially the Piper case) is thus methodologically engineered as the current statement of psychical research itself.

In the final analysis, that statement concerned nothing less than the substance of personal identity. The Myersian notion of the subliminal self is perhaps best understood in the context of contemporary opinion on the unconscious. While psychical research was very much part of a larger matrix of scholarly thought on that subject, it was at the same time taking a considerably different tack from the rest. Janet and others within that wing of the psychological profession concerned with unconscious mental life already tended to view the appearance of submerged levels of personality as pathological and dysfunctional phenomena, fortunately occurring only occasionally. Even then, in Vienna, Sigmund Freud was moving toward a coherent portrayal of the unconscious as the repository of elements deliberately rejected, repressed, by the conscious self.[20] But Myers, the major architect of psychical research's approach to the matter, looked at it from an entirely different perspective. In its own odd way, Myers' work may turn out to be one of the key documents in modern European intellectual history, just as Myers himself may be a much more pivotal figure than he is now acknowledged to be.

Myers did not believe that subliminal states of being erupted only rarely into the waking personality, nor that those states represented that which rational life must eschew, nor that their content and nature were in any sense determined by or even related to that of everyday consciousness at all. In fact, Myers thought not in terms of the "unconscious" as any unitary entity but rather in terms of a multiplicity of levels of selfhood. To him, what was called "normal, waking consciousness" was only one of some yet undetermined number of strata that, clustered together, composed "personality" or "selfhood."

I suggest, then, that the stream of consciousness in which we habitually live is not the only consciousness which exists in connection with our organism. Our habitual or empirical consciousness may consist of a mere selection from a multitude of thoughts and sensations, of which some at least are equally conscious with those that we empirically know. I accord no primacy to my ordinary waking self, except that among my potential selves this one has shown itself the fittest to meet the needs of common life. I hold that it has established no further claim, and that it is perfectly possible that other thoughts, feelings, and memories, either isolated or in continuous connection, may now be actively conscious, as we say, "within me"—in some kind of co-ordination with my organism, and forming some part of my total individuality. I conceive it possible that at some future time, and under changed conditions, I may recollect all; I may assume these various personalities under one single consciousness, in which ultimate and complete consciousness the empirical consciousness which at this moment directs my hand may be only one element out of many.[21]

While the body of Myers' work, culminating in *Human Personality,* is not the most lucidly written, its central ideas are unmistakable. Chief among these is that, to Myers, paranormal or telepathic phenomena were functions of alternate strata or personalities, temporarily in ascendance over the organism. The key point here is that in Myers' view that temporary ascendance was an entirely legitimate one, to be celebrated rather than feared. The subliminal self might reveal itself in hysteria and related forms of pathology to others. To the intrepid Myers, it expressed itself in genius, inspiration, love, joy, mystical illumination, and intense subjective euphoria. It was, in short, the ideal landscape of that "inner life" he had cultivated so long and so assiduously. Myers never developed any real notion, as Freud would later, of the specific anatomy of that region. There is no correlate in his work to the concepts of id, ego, or superego. But he did have a way of describing it. Myers felt he was presenting nothing less than the "indwelling soul, possessing and using the body as a whole."[22]

Myers' own further musings on the subject are convoluted and extremely difficult to simplify. But a tolerably reductionist appreciation of his work reveals one thing clearly. Psychical research, through him, had finally arrived at the intellectual construction targeted from the beginning: a secular version of the soul. All the patient experiments, all the fevered conjecture, all the reasoned debate, and all the bitter in-fighting that had comprised the S.P.R.'s official life had finally yielded a product. It was what those who had initiated the struggle to integrate the core religious sensibility of modern Protestantism into secular culture had dreamed of finding, beginning with the Spiritualists and culminating, now, with Myers. "Subliminal selfhood" was the secular soul.

And it was an entirely novel formulation. It was indeed a version of the soul in that it was described as some mysterious inner part (or parts) of ourselves that distinguished us as categorically superior to other forms of life; it was an "other" part of ourselves entirely. Yet at the same time it was secular in that it was a functioning component of our own earthly organisms, manifest (through telepathic phenomena) in this world. It was in fact an entirely new way of conceptualizing noumenal selfhood.

Actually, the very vagueness of the subliminal dimension of the self, as Myers presented it, may have been one of the qualities that excited those who found themselves interested in psychical research. So much could be read into it. What Myers was saying was that inside each of us is a mysterious but real energy, generating our individual quotients of what we individually believe to be laudable in the human personality. In other words: inside ourselves there are other selves— rather more interesting and better ones. Whatever we wanted to believe we were, we in fact were or could be. The capacity was within us. And that was fact, not an article of faith.

Myers' *Proceedings* articles on subliminal selfhood had aroused a great deal of interest, and the publication of *Human Personality* in book form in 1903 attracted considerable attention.[23] Within the discipline of psychical research, its impact can scarcely be overestimated.[24] Psychical researchers never accepted the entire set of Myers' ideas without reservation. Most significantly, his own belief that the subliminal self probably did survive bodily death was not usually seen to follow with any logical precision even from his own delineation of subliminal selfhood. That delineation, in turn, was often seen as inchoate. But it was precisely the act of filling in the gaps that occupied psychical researchers for the next generation. Indeed, the entire period in the history of psychical research from the turn of the century to the 1920s can justly be called the Age of Myers. His work provided the basic point of departure for discourse on the subject.[25] His notion of subliminal selfhood provided the theoretical framework within or against which subsequent endeavors would be placed. There would really be no other conceptual overview for the discipline until the late 1920s.

This can be seen in the actual content of psychical research as practiced during that interim period. The physical passing of the Cambridge group was almost complete by the early 1900s. Sidgwick had died in 1900, Myers a year later, and Hodgson in 1905. But Mrs. Sidgwick remained, and with Oliver Lodge she served as the S.P.R.'s most important leader and preserved the Cambridge group's (and especially Myers') original orientation toward the field. The major investigative work during that period involved the Piper case (exhaustively) and the famous "cross-correspondences." The latter were parallel or interrelated messages claimed, by the nonprofessional mental mediums who received them, to have come from Myers, Gurney, and other deceased researchers. S.P.R. publications on them revolved almost entirely around the ability of a "split-off" or submerged stratum of personality within the medium to account for such trance-state discourse. Most often, that hypothesis (as opposed to the notion that discarnate spirits were actually communicating) was held to be by far the most plausible. The *Proceedings* for an entire generation were filled with "reports" that were essentially discussions of Myersian principles. Mrs. Sidgwick also reaffirmed that theoretical framework in her discussion of the Piper case. In fact, she tried to incorporate the enormous bulk of material on Mrs. Piper into a book-length treatment explicitly addressed to the theoretical question. Her object, she said, was "to throw light on the working of the trance consciousnesses from a psychological point of view, and, among other things, on the question whether the intelligence that speaks or writes in the trance, and is sometimes in telepathic communication with other minds (whether of the living or of the dead), is other than a phase, or centre of consciousness, of Mrs. Piper herself."[26]

What had happened in psychical research was by then quite clear. Unlike the Spiritualists, psychical researchers had chosen to hold confirmation that any portion of our being survives death in abeyance, pending location of such a portion in the make-up of man himself. They began with various discrete phenomena, then proposed the hypothesis of the telepathic mind to account for them. Eventually, they moved beyond the telepathic mind to what they thought was its true source, submerged strata of personality or subliminal selfhood. This was the actual content of psychical research as it was shown to the public (as, actually, it was screened for the public) in the *Proceedings* and other publications. Essentially, psychical researchers wound up holding the question of the survival of death so far in abeyance that they never really got back to it (as the Spiritualists seemed to have feared they might not). By the Edwardian era, the content of psychical research turned out to be an extended discussion of subliminal selfhood.

What this discipline concerned itself with, then, was the idea of "essence," conceptualized scientifically—or as scientifically as its practitioners could conceptualize it. It offered, at the very most, a confirmation of the idea that human beings are indeed endowed with some essence (i.e., a subliminal self) that is fundamentally "other" than, although contained within, the material body (as demonstrated by the property of telepathy). This was the secular soul. That version of the soul would seem to have been quite distinct from others then current. It did not confirm the survival of death, as did that of the Spiritualists.[27] It included no discussion at all of specific moral codes or prescriptions for behavior, as did those of the churches. It was entirely distinct.

All it offered was the most ringing affirmation of the fact that there was more to humanness than matter, that there were marvelous potentialities deep within us all. The question now was: what sort of response would that stark, elemental message evoke in British society? Was anyone listening? For only if enough were could psychical researcher's audacious attempt to engrave a religious commitment onto a scientific world view succeed.

NOTES

1. "Human Personality in Light of Hypnotic Suggestion," *Proceedings*, vol. 4 (1886–87), pp. 1–24.

2. "On Telepathic Hypnotism and Its Relation to Other Forms of Hypnotic Suggestion," ibid., p. 185.

3. "Peculiarities of Certain Post-Hypnotic States," ibid., pp. 268–323 (quote, p. 323).

4. *The Nineteenth Century,* vol. 20 (November 1886), p. 666.

5. Gauld, *The Founders of Psychical Research,* p. 161.

6. Edmund Gurney, F. W. H. Myers, and Frank Podmore, *Phantasms of the Living,* vols. 1 and 2 (London: The Society for Psychical Research, 1886).

7. His death remains controversial. It has been argued that Gurney, convinced that all his work in and hope for psychical research had come to nothing, committed suicide. This argument is set forth in Trevor Hall's *The Strange Case of Edmund Gurney* (London: Duckworth, 1964). In 1908, and again in 1911, Douglas Blackburn publicly announced that he and G. A. Smith had deceived Gurney and the S.P.R. investigators in the 1882–83 experiments by use of a code. Smith, who became a pioneer in the British film industry, denied the charges. However, Hall posits that Gurney's trip to Brighton that day was motivated by Smith's sister, who, Hall suggests, might have told Gurney at that time what Blackburn would tell the press twenty years later. According to Hall, this revelation, coupled with the criticism leveled at *Phantasms of the Living,* must have pushed the always melancholic Gurney over the edge. The controversy touches on the legitimacy of the important experiments Gurney conducted with Smith on thought transference and mesmerism. It has been addressed at length by current practitioners of psychical research or parapsychology. See, for instance, Gauld's *The Founders of Psychical Research,* pp. 180–85, and his article in the *Journal of the Society for Psychical Research* vol. 43 (1965).

8. The final report of the Committee on the Census of Hallucinations appeared in the *Proceedings,* vol. 10 (1894), pp. 25–394.

9. For material on the Piper case see M. Sage's *Mrs. Piper and the Society for Psychical Research* (London: The Society for Psychical Research, 1903). Her daughter Alta also wrote a biography of her (London, 1929).

10. See the account of the congress published in the *Proceedings,* vol. 6 (1889–90), pp. 171–82.

11. See Mark Baldwin's detailed account, "The London Congress of Experimental Psychology," *The Nation,* September 8, 1892.

12. *The Times* also covered the London congress (August 2, 3, 5, 1892).

13. See the account of the congress published in the *Proceedings,* vol. 8 (1892), pp. 601–11.

14. An expanded version of this paper, written with Alice Johnson and

titled "Experiments in Thought-Transference," appeared in the *Proceedings,* vol. 8, pp. 546–96.

15. An expanded version of this paper, titled "Sensory Automatism and Induced Hallucinations," appeared in the *Proceedings,* vol. 8, pp. 436–535.

16. Accounts of the 1896 congress are preserved in the S.P.R. archives in London *(Internationaler Congress für Psychologie: Vorläufiges Program).* Myers' paper was a reworking of an earlier appraisal of Mrs. Piper in the *Proceedings,* vol. 6, pp. 436–657.

17. Lehman and Hansen of Copenhagen had published in Wundt's *Philosophische Studien* a critique of the G. A. Smith thought-transference experiments, claiming "involuntary whispering" could account for the results.

18. Some present-day workers in this field still consider Myers' book to be "the great classic in the literature of psychical research" (W. H. Salter, *The Society for Psychical Research,* p. 28).

19. This discussion owes a good deal to Alan Gauld, and even more to T. W. Mitchell's article "The Contributions of Psychical Research to Psychotherapeutics" in the *Proceedings,* vol. 45 (1938–39), pp. 175–86.

20. Oddly enough, it was the S.P.R. that introduced Freud to the English reading public. In Myers' article "The Subliminal Consciousness, Chapter 6—The Mechanism of Hysteria," published in the *Proceedings,* vol. 9 (1893–94, pp. 3–128), there is an extended treatment (on pp. 12–15) of J. Breuer and S. Freud's paper "The Psychical Mechanism of Hysterical Phenomena," published in 1893 in *Neurologisches Centralblatt.*

21. "The Subliminal Consciousness," *Proceedings,* vol. 7 (1891–92), pp. 298–355 (quote, p. 301).

22. F. W. H. Myers, *Human Personality and Its Survival of Bodily Death,* vol. 1 (London: Longmans, Green, 1903), p. 34.

23. It was reviewed in *The Nineteenth Century* (vol. 53, 1903); *Mind* (vol. 12, 1903); and *The Hibbert Journal* (vol. 2, 1903).

24. It was analyzed extensively in the 1903 S.P.R. *Proceedings* by Oliver Lodge, William James, and Walter Leaf. Subsequent issues of the *Proceedings* contained large-scale considerations by others.

25. See, for instance, the 1911 *Encyclopedia Britannica's* treatment of psychical research.

26. "A Contribution to the Study of the Psychology of Mrs. Piper's Trance Phenomena," *Proceedings,* vol. 28 (1915), pp. i–xix, 1–652 (quote, p. i).

27. There were, of course, always some Spiritualists in the S.P.R. But it seems that, sooner or later, that residuum's awareness of the distance between

Spiritualism and psychical research required expression. The 1885–86 con-roversy was the first and most important such instance. The next one occurred in the 1920s, when Sir Arthur Conan Doyle spearheaded another Spiritualist assault on the S.P.R.'s leadership (see his *History of Spiritualism* [London, 1926] for a particularly acerbic treatment of psychical research). There is in the S.P.R. archives a circular issued to members decrying the unfairness of his charges in much the same manner as the earlier Spiritualist challenge had been met.

Chapter Six

The Constituency for Psychical Research

THE SECULAR SOUL AND BRITISH CULTURE

There were always those, like Carpenter and Donkin, who would never countenance the use of the term "science" in reference to psychical research. Nevertheless, by the turn of the century others apparently saw reasons to consider the work of the S.P.R. a serious and intellectually legitimate undertaking. So it would seem, at least, from even a cursory glance at the names of some of those who associated themselves with the Society. By 1887, the S.P.R. had numbered among its members eight fellows of the Royal Society,[1] one previous prime minister (W. E. Gladstone), and one future prime minister (Arthur Balfour). Gladstone was said to have called psychical research "the most important work which is being done in the world. By far the most important."[2]

No less striking than the S.P.R.'s ability to interest men of prominence is the success it demonstrated in attracting ordinary, subscription-roll members. The Society's subscription-roll membership was about one hundred fifty at the beginning of 1883. By 1890, it had grown to about seven hundred. By 1900, it was around nine hundred fifty. That figure, roughly six times the Society's original membership, stayed about the same throughout the Edwardian era.[3] Psychical research does seem to have attracted a public of sorts. In fact, that public may even have been fairly sizable. When a House and Finances Committee was formed, it often reported to the council on the demand for the *Proceedings,* both in libraries and in retail bookstores. Sometimes that demand was said to be "considerable," and once it was described as "overwhelming."[4] As has been noted, the findings of psychical research were deliberately disseminated as widely and effectively as possible. Articles in the outside press, as well as retail sales of the *Proceedings* and donations of them to libraries, mechanics' institutes, and the like, were consciously intended to spread the word, as it were. From the beginning, Sidgwick had explicitly spoken of psychical research as an attempt to reach and influence "the common sense of mankind." Public acceptance of their findings had always been the psychical researchers' ultimate goal. Public endorsement of the secular soul had always been their own final measure of success.

How successful might we suspect the psychical researchers were? What sort of public might they plausibly be thought to have attracted? These questions become intriguing if the distinctiveness of the secular soul is recalled. Clearly, anyone who needed or wanted a traditional religious interpretation of human selfhood could turn to the churches. Anyone who felt that traditional interpretation was valuable but suspected that its assertion of the soul's survival of death required empirical confirmation could find his problem addressed more directly in Spiritualism than in psychical research. The secular soul, as opposed to the versions offered by both the churches and the Spiritualists, was rather militantly this-worldly, because that was the only path psychical researchers had seen toward making any proposition of the soul at all meaningful in modern culture (i.e., vis-à-vis "Science"). Put simply, who could have needed or wanted *this* version? What factors in British life might have been promoting receptivity toward *this* one?

The psychical researchers themselves, the actual investigators of the S.P.R., were practicing intellectuals. Their very professions involved the formation, processing, and dissemination of ideas. By 1900, after a generation of work, they had an interpretation ready for public consumption. But success in what might be called the distributive phase of their work would mean that nonintellectuals, people in social strata where ideas were not stock-in-trade in and of themselves, were finding something meaningful in the secular soul. The idea had to be more than merely credible to attain the level of popular endorsement the S.P.R.'s leaders wanted. In fact, it had to be more than probable, or even demonstrable. Any number of ideas, after all, are always both demonstrably true and demonstrably useless in society as a whole. For the secular soul to succeed in the marketplace of ideas, it had to be both credible and consequential. It had to matter, had to offer something needed in daily life.

The intellectuals in the S.P.R. had seen the idea of the soul ranged against those of science, and in psychical research had sought a viable compromise. For them "the soul" and "science," purely as abstractions or cerebral constructions, had in a sense provided countervailing pressures from which the concept of the secular soul had been produced. But for laymen personally meaningful ideas were less often the result of sheer, focused cerebration than reflections of the tangible affairs of daily life. Among people who took the secular soul seriously, there must have been some sort of experiential referents of the abstractions "soul" and "science" in daily life, perceived realities that somehow drew or even compelled them to psychical research. The real heart of the story of psychical research is the manner in which its message related to the palpable circumstances of British lives.

It is possible to find and examine some of the lives into which psychical research was warmly welcomed. The S.P.R.'s lay membership was divided into two categories. Associates paid one guinea yearly, could attend general meetings, could use (but not borrow from) the S.P.R. library, and could receive the *Proceedings* and the *Journal* free of charge. Members, on the other hand, paid two guineas yearly, could hold any office in the Society, could vote for council members, could attend both general and business meetings, could borrow freely from the library, and could receive the *Proceedings,* the *Journal,* and any other publication issued by the Society free of charge.

Members were manifestly more involved with psychical research. After 1900, that could only have meant they found personal meaning in what has been called the secular soul, because after 1900 that concept (or cluster of concepts) was unmistakably the gist of psychical research. Thus if the population of members is screened for those who retained that standing for a minimum of five consecutive years after 1900, it is possible to locate a nucleus of people who with some certainty can be thought to have taken the secular soul very seriously indeed. Examining a sample of such people might reveal something about the sorts of daily realities or pressures that drew people to psychical research during its Myersian age.

Of course, caution must be exercised. The number of people meeting sampling criteria who left enough personal records to permit some reconstruction of their lives is quite small. In addition, the biographical material on even that small number is often incomplete. Any inferences drawn from such materials about the lay constituency for psychical research would have to be regarded as highly tentative. In addition, it is obvious that the records available would be on middle- or upper-class individuals only, because only fairly well-to-do and well-educated types could afford the Society's dues and read its often highly technical reports. Therefore, such suggestions as are made about the secular soul's attraction could refer only to those social groups, although the constituency for psychical research may have extended beyond them.

Nevertheless, while the data at hand can yield no more than preliminary hypotheses, examining them is worth the effort. It is not unreasonable to expect that so provocative a notion as the secular soul might have been connected to a fairly provocative set of lives.

MEMBERS: "THE PROFESSIONAL WORLD"

Sir Alfred Scott-Gatty

Alfred Scott-Gatty was a man who valued the innocence of childhood.

His own was probably quite happy. He was born in 1847 in Ecclesfield, Yorkshire, to the Rev. Alfred Gatty, D.D., and Margaret Scott.[5] His mother was the daughter and heir of Rev. John Scott, D.D. (sometime private secretary to Horatio, Viscount Nelson), and seems to have exerted a considerable influence over young Alfred. He was educated at Marlborough and Christ's College, Cambridge, but returned to his mother for the initiation of his true calling. In 1892 he added, by royal license, her surname to his own.

Scott-Gatty's mother was editor of *Aunt Judy's Magazine,* a pastiche of children's songs, games, and jokes laced with moral maxims that reflected the oft-mentioned idealization of childhood associated with the Victorian era. Alfred was a music lover, and in 1867 he published his first composition in his mother's serial. It was entitled "Aunt Judy's Gallop," and heralded a successful career in music. Scott-Gatty was twenty when he penned this first exercise in musical juvenilia. He was still turning it out nearly thirty years later. From 1867 to 1895 he wrote over four hundred fifty songs, representative titles of which may indicate something of the nature of his creative energies.[6]

The year 1869 was one of genuine inspiration. He produced, among many others, "Tune the Old Cow Died Of," "Heigh-Ho Daisies!," "Naughty Tom," "Bobbie! Bobbie!," "Going to School," "Tommie! Tommie!," "The Sneezing Song," and, returning to a favored motif, "Robin! Robin!" By 1871 he had added to his credits "The Child Angels," "Forget Me Not," and "Will You Walk a Little Faster?" By 1872 he seems to have turned toward deeper thoughts with "Cruel Hours," "Farewell! Farewell!," "She Was But a Child," and "Sweet Was the Life Lived with Thee." But the true Scott-Gatty spirit returned in 1873 with the triumphant "Ha! Ha! Ha!" In 1874 he married, an event that may have helped catalyze that year's "I Don't Know How It Came About," "I'm Not That Sort of Man," and, after a year's conjugal experience, "Tarry, Tarry, Ere Ye Marry." By 1881 his credits extended to "Naughty Hugh," "Grumbling Joe," and "Do All the Good That You Can."

The last-named tune Scott-Gatty donated to a Serjeant Manners of the London Police Force, to be sung at "People's Entertainments." His sense of civic responsibility very probably had much to do with his eventual knighthood, in 1894. He devoted considerable time to the production of children's shows and comic operettas *(Rumpelstiltskin, The Three Bears)* for charity. One such effort, entitled *Not At Home,* included a song called "Life Is Not All Roses." And indeed, even for a man of Scott-Gatty's talents, it wasn't. Sooner or later, even children and artists must face the sordid realities of Commerce.

Scott-Gatty committed to his personal manuscript collection a carefully detailed account of an imbroglio with the publishing industry indicating that in his case confronting those realities was particularly traumatic. In addition to the record of his professional output, that account constitutes the entirety of his manuscript collection. Apparently, this was the only biographical incident he deemed meaningful enough to preserve for posterity.

On April 13, 1869, Scott-Gatty signed a contract with the publishing firm of Messrs. Robert Cocks and Co. in which he agreed to supply them for three years with eight original compositions per year, for the sum of £100 yearly. On receipt of a £100 advance, he gave Cocks and Co. the right to publish twelve previously written songs, and the exclusive right to publish in folio size twelve other titles. All of these were issued between 1869 and 1872, under Scott-Gatty's own name. In 1870, however, he agreed with Messrs. John Boosey and Co. to supply that firm with eight manuscripts per year for two years (also at £100 yearly), these songs to appear under the nom de plume "Conyer Vaughn." A further agreement, more favorable to the composer, was reached with Boosey in 1872. For each of the following three years, Scott-Gatty was to supply eight songs under his own name for £200 yearly and a royalty of £10 per one thousand copies after four thousand had been sold. But there were complications.

In February of 1875, Scott-Gatty wanted a renewal of his contract with Boosey on the previous terms. To advance the negotiations, he sold the firm the whole of his reversionary royalty on a briskly selling song ("One Morning Oh So Early") for £100. But that July, John Boosey announced his desire to discontinue relations upon expiration of the current contract. "I replied," recorded Scott-Gatty, "that I had sold

One Morning Oh So Early solely to renew that contract and that I expected him to hold to the agreement. But on August 20, 1875, John Boosey wrote threatening to repudiate the agreement owing to Messrs. Robert Cocks and Co. having brought out two songs *under my own name.*" Confused, Scott-Gatty explained to Boosey that those songs were part of the old (1869–1872) agreement signed with Cocks. Cocks' actions, he said, could not be prevented, nor did they have any relevance at all to the current contractual negotiations with Boosey. But Boosey claimed Cocks' actions violated Scott-Gatty's 1872–1875 agreement with his firm, by which Boosey and Co. had exclusive right to the Scott-Gatty name. "Of course I cannot renew it," he argued, "in the face of this outbreak from my rival publisher Cocks."

Scott-Gatty was by this time rather seriously distressed. Boosey wanted him to pressure Cocks into foregoing the use of his name. The Cocks firm was using only material covered during the term of its own agreement with Scott-Gatty, and only in the manner contractually stipulated. But Boosey was, it would seem, taking advantage of a loophole. Apparently, it had never been specified in the Cocks contract how long the publisher could continue releasing material delivered by the composer between 1869 and 1872. Scott-Gatty had, as Boosey knew, an operetta he badly wanted published. Boosey was not only denying his own firm's services but forcing the composer to antagonize another as well.

Scott-Gatty obliged by writing to Cocks. "I know you have a legal mind and are better acquainted in the usages of the musical business than I am. [He was twenty-eight at the time and had been composing for eight years.] I therefore am about to trouble you with a little difficulty because *you* are the cause of it." But Cocks was not helpful. "Much as we deplore the position you are placed in," he said, "we must emphatically decline to yield the point upon any terms. We should lose self-respect were we to do so. . . . The request is a most unreasonable and unfair one on their part, and such as no House of independent feeling could entertain for a moment." Boosey's next letter was even more discouraging. "I beg to give you notice that I will not renew the agreement unless you undertake that Cocks shall publish no more songs under your own name. I must remind you that when we made our agreement three years ago it was never contemplated that Cocks' or any other House should publish your songs even under a *nom de plume*." He closed by stating unctuously, "I have no wish to interfere with your power of disposing of the operetta elsewhere."

Alfred Scott-Gatty, purveyor of simple tunes, was even then quite baffled by the situation. He was, it seemed, helplessly trapped in a tug of war over the commercial exploitation of his own name. But Boosey's plan should have been clear to anyone when, with no discussion of the operetta, he offered to buy out the reversionary royalties on all songs covered by his agreement with the composer. Following that transaction, Boosey informed Scott-Gatty, their dealings would be quite finished.

Abjectly, Scott-Gatty crawled to his tormentor. He explained that he was simply unable to stop Cocks, then announced brightly that his operetta was almost finished. ("I should be happy to let you see it with a view to a separate arrangement, unless you choose to decline any new dealings with me. Perhaps you will kindly answer me on this point.") But Boosey's response was a flat offer of £150 for reversionary interest on all remaining songs in their agreement, with no mention of the operetta at all. Desperate, Scott-Gatty wrote to an attorney named Crowdy and requested counsel. ("The terms contained are simply insulting.") But Crowdy was about to go abroad, and could not help. Scott-Gatty was alone, and quite beaten.

On November 20, 1876, he wrote a letter to Boosey that described the state he finally realized the publisher had manipulated him into.

> I have been in hopes of hearing from you in the settlement of our affairs. I think you must understand my position. I am so to speak stranded as to my musical affairs. . . . I have as yet done nothing with anyone re the future and I cannot do so until I have settled with you. Meantime,

Christmas and its attendant "fairies" in the form of bills are quickly and surely approaching.

Then he presented his analysis of the entire incident. Using terminology he had employed previously, he compared the Booseys of the musical field ("Professionals") to his own ilk ("Amateurs"), the struggling artists. His wording strongly suggests that this was not the first such clash he had witnessed between the two.

> I am aware that the *Professional* world has been the cause of my misfortunes, and you have lent a willing ear to their remarks on me and such as me—the position of Professionals and Amateurs is easily given—the former live by their art, the latter live *for* their Art.

There is no record of whether or not Boosey got the reversionary rights he wanted, or whether the operetta was published on a cut-rate deal. Scott-Gatty, of course, eventually found other publishers. But even with the education Boosey had provided, he apparently never trusted his own ability to deal with them. Further relations with the "Professionals" were undertaken through solicitors.

A profound innocence may be required of a man who spends his twentieth to his forty-eighth year immersed in children's ditties. In Scott-Gatty's case, that innocence may even have constituted the essence of the man; certainly it was the wellspring of his art. But there were elements of the world in which he functioned that appraised him differently, and hungrily. Scott-Gatty seems to have recognized in the Boosey affair that the real forces of marketing and financial muscle in his own field were quite capable of treating him as a mere pawn, his name itself a commodity. To the "Professionals," the real Alfred Scott-Gatty was not an Artist but an Asset.

In later years, the composer chose to attach himself to a social environment almost as far removed from that of commerce as can be imagined. In 1880 he was appointed Rouge Dragon Pursuivant of Arms at the Royal College of Heralds, becoming York Herald in 1886 and Garter King-at-Arms in 1904. While attending to the symbolic accoutrements of nobility, he affiliated himself with the Society for Psychical Research. Tales of the secular soul held his ear from 1910 to 1917. The following year he died.

Selwyn Francis Edge

The life of entrepreneurship that Scott-Gatty found so poisonous was, on the other hand, utterly exhilarating to Selwyn Francis Edge. Edge was a man with a vision, and the account he gives of his life is one long record of triumph over obstacles the world placed in the way of its realization. In the most literal sense possible, the life he describes was a romance of the open road.[7]

He was born in Sydney, New South Wales, in 1868. Little is recorded of his social background (he ignored it and his family entirely in his autobiography). But, whatever his family's status was, they apparently didn't feel it would suffer too much by leaving Australia. In 1871, the Edges immigrated to England, where Selwyn experienced a rather difficult childhood. He suffered from a serious respiratory ailment and poor health in general. At fourteen, a weakling unable to play most normal adolescent games, he violated the advice of doctors and tried to build up his strength with a bicycle.[8] In this he was successful, and grew into a robust man. It would not be the only time his conviction of superior inner qualities would be pitted against, and victorious over, hostile outside forces.

His family had intended him to pursue a career in the Army, but Edge rejected that scenario and instead took a job with a bicycle firm (Rudge's) in Holborn, London. However, in the bicycle trade, he found something akin to the regimentation he had tried to avoid by sidestepping the military. Edge was sent out as a commercial traveler by Rudge's to sell their machines, but he insisted on devoting his time to racing bicycles rather than personally hawking them. He made a name for himself as a long-distance cyclist, submitting to the firm that his own notoriety contributed heavily to sales.

That formula proved successful. The cycle business was booming. By 1883 Edge had become first Rudge's London manager, then its general manager. Yet he could not settle comfortably into the niche he had carved out in the bicycle trade. He was already aware of a new, far more exciting vehicle: the motorcar. He had been introduced to it by the Frenchman Ferdinand Charron, an old friend and rival from competitive cycling. Purchasing a French car, he entered the Paris-Marseilles race of 1896 and finished second. At that point, Selwyn Francis Edge decided that the motorcar was in fact the coming glory of the age. [9]

He bolted Rudge's, executive position and all, for the Dunlop Tyre Company because they were interested in developing pneumatic tires, which he knew motorcars would eventually need. The chairman of Dunlop, Harvey Du Cross, recognized Edge's value as a bicycle racer, but he was unenthusiastic about cars on the grounds that legal restrictions would thwart their marketability in Britain. Edge champed at the bit, casting about for a sponsor who would help him promote the new invention. He finally found one in Montague Napier, grandson of the founder of one of Britain's largest general engineering firms. Napier experimented on Edge's French machine, making alterations on the steering mechanism and the radiator. Edge concluded that the improved vehicle promised big things. Somehow, he talked Du Cross into financing, for a share in the profits, a pathfinding venture: the Napier Motor Vehicle Company, composed of Napier and Edge.

The attraction the motorcar held for Edge was a curious one. He was not mechanically adept (he was, in fact, atypically maladroit among motorists in that regard). [10] And, having attained executive status and, presumably, financial reward at Rudge's, he could have remained either there or at Dunlop's if those were his only drives. What life with the motorcar offered, as Edge describes it, was a struggle between genuine entrepreneurial vision and its primeval antagonists, the obstructionism of officialdom and generalized social inertia. He returns again and again in his autobiography to the herculean

efforts required of motoring pioneers to survive the hostility and my-
opia of British society.

First of all, there was the law. Legislation was passed in 1896
permitting motorcars on British roads at up to twelve miles per hour,
but Edge claimed "it did little more than permit motor vehicles to be
used on the highways under very difficult conditions" because "from
the outset the police saw a field for great activity."[11] Low speed limits
and police action aside, there was the backwardness of British industry
(contrasted with Continental industry) in supplying the new enterprise,
even a reluctance to pave roads intended for horse traffic. But, worst of
all, there were "the yokels." Edge devotes an entire chapter to them,
recounting how people placed nails and broken glass in front of cars;
how he himself was horsewhipped by the driver of a cart he passed; how
he was struck in the head with a large piece of ice thrown by an enraged
horseman; how "this sort of bombardment increased ten-fold if a car or
motor-cycle happened to need adjustment or should break down at the
roadside"; how he once even received a written death threat.[12]

But it was precisely the conquest of those difficulties that Edge
relished. He goes on to relate that the horsewhip-wielder's weapon was
seized and used on himself; that the ice-chucker was thrashed and
stripped naked in freezing weather; that Selwyn Francis Edge, swim-
ming upstream all the way, persisted and triumphed—just as he had
when, despite doctors' orders, he had clambered onto his first bicycle.
Edge contended that his triumph reflected distinctive, almost superhu-
man capabilities, rare even within the narrow ranks of intrepids involved with motorcars in Britain. For he was—first, last, and always—
a racing man.

He used the same argument with Napier that he had used at
Rudge's to justify, in the entrepreneurial context, his passion for racing, with the addendum that technological advance began in the racing
pit. In fact, the bulk of his autobiography is devoted to his exploits on
the track. First, there was the Thousand Mile Trial of 1900, from
London to Bristol and back. This was followed by his first great *tour de
force* in the Gordon-Bennett Race of 1902. Edge describes almost lov-

ingly each catastrophe that befell him in that epic contest. These included a cracked cylinder head, defective speed-gear pinions, a damaged reverse gear, four simultaneously punctured tires, Napier's personal withdrawal of confidence, and a host of somewhat more minor setbacks. None could prevent his victory, the first by an Englishman. And that was but a prelude to his great, crowning achievement: the twenty-four hour Brooklands run in 1906.

The construction of the Brooklands racing track had been undertaken in order to circumvent the British government's official restrictions on the use of public thoroughfares for racing. Edge participated in its inaugural run, an endurance test, in order to "get it off to a good start" as well as to demonstrate his and Napier's new six-cylinder engine. In twenty-four nonstop hours he drove 1,581 miles, averaging nearly sixty-six miles per hour. The record he set, which stood for eighteen years, was a particular source of pride to Edge. He noted that at the time most people thought human life could not exist at that speed for so long, that the human mind lost its reason under those conditions.[13] But Edge had been proving the world's estimations of his inner capacities wrong for some time.

However, all good things must come to an end. In 1908 Edge decided that "the products of England could best be served in the future by scientific research into weaknesses which racing had disclosed and experience had shown." Why that should so suddenly be the case he never disclosed. But he did admit to feeling somewhat alien among the sort of men racing was now attracting.

> Then again, the professional element had been slowly but surely creeping into motor racing. It was one thing for those who, like myself, held in their hands the life-strings of some important manufacturing firm, to drive the products of their factories; but it was quite another to import into the racing circle drivers who piloted their cars purely for reward, and without thought of the sport itself.[14]

Coterminous with this realization of a pygmy invasion of his own field ("I could never fathom a mentality which sees in motoring nothing more than a means of transport") was Edge's involvement with the Society for Psychical Research, which he first joined as a member in 1910. In 1912 he sold out his share in the Napier Motor Vehicle Company and retired to a farm. His life, however, was by no means over. He slipped easily into the role of revered elder figure of the motor-car movement, and held it until his death in 1940. He lectured to automobile clubs, appeared at motorcar exhibitions, and held honorific posts, including the presidency of the Association of Pioneer Motorists.[15] He was not at all reluctant to criticize the industry he had loved, complaining that manufacturers had become too interested in marketing cars on the basis of their "smart" and "speedy" looks, at the expense of their "dignity."[16] And modern motorists were in his opinion an inferior lot. In an address to the Lancashire Automobile Club he observed sadly that "anybody with the money can buy and drive away a car."[17] Even in retirement, however, he continued to race— motorboats.

Sir Walter Henry Cowan

Walter Henry Cowan began writing his autobiography while sitting in a P.O.W. camp in northern Italy in 1942. He had retired from the Navy nine years before World War II began, but the Admiralty had bowed to his urgent entreaties and reactivated him. They apparently shared at least to some degree his own belief that, even at age sixty-nine, there was fight left in the old war-horse yet. Those who knew him personally knew that fighting was quite literally what he lived for.[18]

Cowan's career in the Navy was, to say the least, eventful. In fact, spectacular is a more apt description. He first saw action on the Red Sea and throughout Africa, where he participated in both the Omdurman assault and the Fashoda incident. A full captain by 1906, he fought at Jutland in 1916. In 1920 he was in command of the entire British naval force in the Baltic during the anti-Bolshevik operations. An admiral by 1927, he was commander in chief of all naval forces in

North America, South America, and the West Indies. In 1929 he was made first and principal aide-de-camp to the king, and the following year he retired. But when the war broke out in 1939 the Admiralty found Walter Henry Cowan pounding on its door, requesting recommission.

In the Cowan collection in the National Maritime Museum, there is a looseleaf copy of a poem by Sir Henry Newbolt included among Cowan's own writings.[19]

> To set the Cause above renown
> To love the Game beyond the prize
> To honour though you strike him down
> The foe that comes with fearless eyes.
> To hold the life of Battle good
> And dear the land that gave you birth
> And dearer still the brotherhood
> That binds the Brave of all the Earth.

Cowan was the type of man who appreciated sentiments like these. His character was of a sort not easily understood today. The designation "professional soldier" does not really provide the right nuances. He was, rather, pure warrior. The nature of the man is indicated far better by his own words than by anything said about him. Particularly self-revelatory are his discussions of happy days campaigning against African slave traders.

> After a period of constant odd jobs mostly on shore with the ship going off somewhere else, there were a lot of villages to be routed out. I enjoyed myself there. One good day I well remember—we went out at dawn—Murray Lockhart, son of the commander in chief India, and I— marched thirty-nine miles, burnt five villages, and brought back twenty-six prisoners tied neck and neck.[20]

> They [slave dhows] were full of tricks. . . . They might heave-to and make signs of surrender, and then if—as a sailor would—you ran alongside to leeward, they would drop their sail so that it fell over the boat and then stab and shoot through it. A very gallant sailor Fife Fegen got

caught that way, more than half his crew disabled and then was for days drifting about in the direct heat and very short of surgical stores and water. The wounded were in a desperate state of maggots and gangrene when they were picked up. It was all great fun for a young man.[21]

Wherever we went on either coast those little wars and their repercussions sprang up, though compared with these two last wars we have got to the end of since those African scrambles were just "chicken feed." Still, they were a long way better than nothing for a young man.[22]

There is certainly one charge that could never be leveled at Walter Henry Cowan: he was no dilettante in warfare. He experienced a great deal of it, and in fact seems to have considered combat the staff of life itself. His fondest memories even of cadethood involved combat, especially the occasional gang fights among trainees. ("I can remember feeling a certain amount of pride in having had to have my eye lanced by the doctor in one of them.")[23] To professional soldiers, military action is the continuation of policy by other means, calculated as rationally as possible and implemented by organized, large-scale groupings of men. To Cowan, it was a personal matter: himself vs. The Enemy, man to man. The professionals plotted British naval strategy in World War I, and quite successfully if success is judged in terms of the practical contribution of naval operations to the overall contest between nations. But that was not exactly how Cowan saw it. "There was rather an aching, flat sort of feeling about it all," he noted glumly, "as beyond dominating them and denying the seas to them, we had never properly thrashed them out in the open."[24]

The sense of thwarted drives expressed in that passage is evoked several times in Cowan's writings. They record a number of instances when he felt the military was insufficiently responsive to a true warrior's nature, when he felt they made insufficient use of his talents. In fact, contretemps with military authorities dotted his career from the beginning. Some were trivial, others were not. All revolved around his irrepressible desire to join the fray, wherever and whatever it might be.

On the *Redbreast,* during his days in Africa, he contracted a serious case of dysentery and was temporarily sent home. But he begged to be returned to his station when he learned that two *Redbreast* officers had been killed in action against "some tribe that had been misbehaving." Unable to reverse the medical officer's decision but constitutionally incapable of sitting out the impending punitive operation, he resorted to pulling strings.[25] He would, however, require considerably longer strings the next time he acted on a warrior's instincts instead of established operating procedure.

During the Boer War the British Navy was involved only in transport. That hardly provided enough action to satisfy Cowan. In some manner never (understandably) disclosed in detail, he contrived to leave his ship, the *Barossa,* and participate in the conflict as Kitchener's aide in charge of horses. "It was a good life," he recalled, "getting somewhere near to the bottom of four horses and seeing a lot of mixed warfare.[99] But the Admiralty was not amused by his abrupt switch in services. While never citing the specific violations he was accused of, Cowan duly records that "charges" were brought against him. In fact, it required Kitchener and Lord Roberts' personal intervention to bail him out.[26] But if naval authorities were critical of his procedures, he could be equally critical of theirs.

Cowan claimed that the Royal Navy's honor and integrity had been impugned by the fact that Kitchener perished while in its care, adding that specific charge to his generalized complaint about the Navy's failure to provide a truly satisfying slugfest with the Germans during World War I. Finally, shortly after the war, an incident occurred in which he felt his own honor to have been appraised in cavalier fashion by the military authorities. His ship, *Falcon,* collided at night with a fishing trawler without lights. One of the fishermen was killed. Although the incident occurred within the three-mile commercial fishing limit, Cowan insisted the vessel was a poacher. He was absolved of any charge of misconduct by a naval court of enquiry, but no official naval intervention was offered to prevent the trawler's owners from bringing charges in civil court. Cowan was astonished that the Navy would leave a man like himself to the tender mercies of a nonmilitary tribunal, and said so.[27] But it was during his participation in the anti-Bolshevik operations that he made his sharpest criticism of all those staff officers/bureaucrats/politicians who had never really known quite how to channel his energies. He achieved considerable notoriety by publicly, albeit futilely, insisting that the Royal Navy relieve the beseiged garrison at Kronstadt.[28]

It would be a gross misrepresentation to suggest that Cowan was in any sense anti-Navy. He did, however, experience some difficulty in adjusting to its estimation of the degree to which his personal imperatives could be allowed expression. He was in a very real sense a harnessed creature, and he knew it.

However inconvenient in a peripatetic life, he was a member of the Society for Psychical Research from prior to 1901 to 1914.

Richard H. Norris

R. H. Norris, a professor of physiology in the School of Medicine at the University of Birmingham, was convinced he was a genius. His problem was convincing the rest of the world. Norris' specialty was the physiopathology of the blood. His own research in that area (which he augmented by personally innovating improvements in photographic equipment) yielded, he thought, clear proof of a startling fact.[29] In August 1877, he claimed to have discovered that "there existed elements in the blood which have been entirely overlooked and this because they had the same color and refractive index as the matter on which they lay." Norris believed he had uncovered a third corpuscle. The rest of his career as a physiologist consisted of one long attempt to secure recognition of that achievement by his profession.

The first person he chose to inform of his discovery was the major textbook author in the field, Michael Foster. Announcing that he had found corpuscles in the blood that were invisible under ordinary conditions of observation, he asked Foster which practicing physiologists to approach with his findings. Foster suggested a Dr. Sanderson, who agreed that Norris had found something but wasn't entirely sure what it was. Sanderson referred him to Thomas Huxley, and at that point Norris' fortunes took a decided turn for the worse.

Huxley pooh-poohed him on the grounds that in twenty-five years of work, using the best microscopes in existence, he, Huxley, had never seen anything like what Norris described. Norris replied that this was attributable to the substance's refractive index, but Huxley remained unimpressed. Norris "left without having made any favorable impression."[30]

Huxley's disapproval probably had more than a little to do with the reception afforded Norris' work by the agency that standardized scientific knowledge in Britain, the Royal Society. They returned his paper (and accompanying photographs) unopened. But he did find a forum for the promulgation of his views. He gave two demonstrations at the Royal College of Physicians, and two more at the British Medical Association. Emboldened, he sent his paper off to the Royal Society a second time. Again they rejected it, without explanation, as "unsuitable."

As Norris knew, the discovery of a third corpuscle would indeed entail a radical revision of the physiological profession's understanding of a key area. He insisted, however, that this new corpuscle's existence was the only logical conclusion to be derived from his findings. But as it turned out, those findings could be related to the physiologists' storehouse of knowledge without drastically challenging any prevailing paradigm. In 1879 Ernest Hart, editor of *The British Medical Journal*, asked Norris to give a special demonstration to his wife, who was then studying medicine in Paris. The following year Mrs. Hart published an appraisal of Norris' work in *The London Medical Record*. In it, she submitted that what Norris had seen were red corpuscles in a state of partial decomposition. Norris, she suggested, had misinterpreted them as colorless because they were affected by his method of isolating and photographing them. She went on to argue that those corpuscles underwent post-mortem alterations prior to taking part in the formation of fibrosis.

Norris was furious. He claimed to have realized from the beginning that the substance he had found participated decisively in the formation of fibrous networks causing coagulation. Mrs. Hart, he charged, had stolen the portion of his work that the physiological profession could find useful while unfairly dismissing the less convenient aspect of it (i.e., the insistence that an entirely new type of corpuscle had been located). To add insult to injury, his own book on the subject was unfavorably reviewed in Hart's journal. And in 1882 Mrs. Hart again took credit for the correct interpretation of Norris' findings (of which he himself, according to her, had been incapable) in *The Quarterly Journal of Microscopic Studies*.

The bitterness Norris felt at "this woman, who had from me all the methods she used" never abated. But he came to realize that Mrs. Hart's actions were only symptomatic of a larger malaise. Scientific knowledge, he concluded, was only irregularly knowledge in any epistemologically defensible sense. It was, rather, merely the end product of intellectual labor conducted under socially controlled conditions. What passed for knowledge was simply that which pleased an elite (Huxley, the Royal Society) that had arrogated unto itself supreme responsibility for passing judgment on truth and falsehood. Mrs. Hart had pleased it, and so her interpretation of his findings found its way into the textbooks while his own would not. To Norris, the moral of the story was that "there is no true enthusiasm for Science in this country—it is simply a strife for position and place."[31]

The depth of Norris' conviction in this matter is perhaps best indicated by his willingness to sustain a close relationship with an American chemist, John J. Gamgee. That relationship seems to have revolved almost entirely around each man's reinforcement of the other's sense of having been martyred in the cause of science by, ironically, professional scientists.

Gamgee was considerably more vitriolic on the subject than Norris. The Englishman considered himself thwarted by a scientific establishment whose primary interest was not the discovery and dissemination of truth but the protection of its own views and status. The American broadened that critique to include an indictment of a general system of class privileges, which the allocation of rewards and recognition in the scientific professions reflected.[32] Gamgee's research had been on the compression and combination of gases. He insisted that he had discovered therein the key to understanding the movement of the bloodstream and, through it, the source of all human mobility. Gamgee thought Norris' third corpuscle combined with oxygen to propel the bloodstream. He also believed, quite sincerely, that "the blood moves the body and not the body the blood."[33] When Norris saw the reception accorded those views, he decided he had found a true brother in arms.

The Norris-Gamgee alliance was intended, in the latter's words, "to sweep away before the end of the century all the stupid ideas of the correlation of forces, transformation and conservation of energy and the science of thermodynamics."[34] This pair actually plotted and carried out subversive warfare against the professional "cliques" that blocked recognition of their accomplishments. The strategy was that each would champion the other's cause by expressing dismay to colleagues at the treatment the other had received from his profession.[35] But the cliques prevailed. Neither Norris nor Gamgee's brilliance was ever acknowledged, and science to this day does not admit that a third corpuscle exists in the bloodstream or that the blood moves the body. By 1894, Norris and Gamgee were ready to abandon the world of professional science altogether in favor of a commercial venture. Together they formed the Birmingham Dry Collodion Plate Film Co., Ltd., to exploit Norris' photographic innovations. But in this too they failed.

Richard Norris, rebuffed by both professional scientists in his original field and by market forces in photography, took to psychical research with a passion. He was an S.P.R. member from 1900 until 1915, and his manuscript collection contains reams of written material on the subject (including his own question-and-answer dialogue with the entire corpus of F. W. H. Myers' work). On the basis of published S.P.R. researches and his own independent work, he arrived at certain conclusions. He generally agreed with Myers on "the substratum of consciousness." To Norris, that substratum was the repository of "will, emotion, fear, love, joy, hatred, etc." While acknowledging that "the essential nature of those we may never understand," he felt we could "be content with knowing them as ultimate facts of our experience, with the thought that those are the essence of our selfhood."[36]

Norris also shared Myers' conviction of an afterlife, but he went considerably beyond Myers to an unqualified affirmation of spirit intercourse with human beings. In fact, he decided that there were distinct brands of spirit-human rapport: the "afferent" (establishment of low-level relations between spirit and the "supersensuous" region of an individual's mind) and the "efferent" (far more intense, symbiotic relationships between man and spirit).[37] To Norris, the spirits both inspired and drew inspiration from human counterparts in the efferent stage of rapport. In that state, man's awareness was simultaneously rendered immortal (through absorption by imperishable entities) and expanded beyond the limits imposed by his own physiological mechanisms (through injections from those imperishable entities).

Brilliance was brilliance, after all.

Geoffrey Le Mesurier Mander

Geoffrey Le Mesurier Mander has been described as "a typical English radical," representing "what is surely an English phenomenon—the presence in left-wing political parties of men who propose and support measures in opposition to their own private interests, and at variance with their 'privileged' background."[38] To him, the radical tradition simply meant the struggle for "certain human rights, among them equality of opportunity and a basic minimum standard of life for all."[39] Unfortunately, he was to find serious constraints on his ability to put those principles into operation.

Mander's father was the owner of Mander Brothers, an old, well-established manufacturing firm in Wolverhampton that turned out paint, varnish, and printing ink. He educated young Geoffrey (born in 1882) at Harrow and Trinity College, Cambridge, and encouraged in him a sense of responsibility and interest in public life. When the elder Mander died in 1900 (while mayor of Wolverhampton), Geoffrey inherited the estate. In later years, he would point with pride to the benefits he brought to workers in his employ. But from the beginning, Mander wanted to function (radically) on a larger scale. He was called to the bar and joined the Oxford circuit, but he never practiced. His consuming interest was not law but politics, into which he threw himself during the general election of 1906.

Mander's radical principles were, he insists in his autobiography, the only source of inspiration for political action he ever knew. At first, he perceived the chief antagonists of those principles to be the Conservatives. In 1906 he helped Liberal parliamentary candidates in the Kingswinford Division of Staffordshire and in East Wolverhampton. He even supported a Labour candidate in West Wolverhampton, where there was no Liberal to run against the Conservative incumbent. "My action caused great consternation in Conservative circles in the neighborhood," he remarked, "and I found myself cut in the hunting field by some of them."[40]

In return for his services, Mander was awarded a magistracy on the Wolverhampton bench (which he retained until he was seventy-five) by the new Liberal government of 1906. In 1909 he became a member of the Wolverhampton town council, where he fought for an increase in the council-employed workers' minimum wage. A period of ill health kept him out of World War I until 1916, when he served in the Royal Flying Corps. But by 1919 he had serious misgivings about whether or not the Liberal Party was really the place for a man of his advanced political views. He had been seriously upset when the Liberal government led the nation into war in 1914 because the staff conversations with the French that preceded that move had never been made known to the country, or even to many cabinet members.

Mander toyed with the idea of joining the Labour Party. However, his qualms about the wisdom of operating from within the Liberal fold were, at this particular juncture, assuaged by party professionals. He decided to stand for office in a Midlands constituency where he could expect some Labour votes. To secure that and additional support, he began churning out a series of succinct little statements of his ideas, entitled *Mander's Monthly Messages*. These pamphlets consisted of attacks, in highly simplified language, on the policies of the coalition government.

Mander was quite eclectic in his interests, and never at a loss for solutions to problems. The June 1921 edition of his publication announced: "Things were cheap seven years ago because we had FREE TRADE." In July, he exhorted: "If you want *Good Trade, Regular Work, Cheap Living, Peace and Quietness,* THE LIBERAL IS YOUR MAN!" Regarding Ireland, he denounced "the use of force." On foreign policy in general he stood foursquare for "peace and goodwill," which he expected would "develop our export trade again and create a demand in the great towns for the food which the countryside supplies" (January and March 1922). On agrarian problems in general, he felt the answer was to be found in an agricultural laborers' trade union. He believed such a union "would lead to country people's developing their minds and enjoying leisure time in things like Village Clubs, Women's Institutes, lectures, concerts, whist drives, dances, football and cricket matches" (March 1922). At the time, Geoffrey Mander was nothing if not confident.

But he lost in 1921. He lost again in 1923. And he lost again in the general election of 1924. By 1929, when he finally entered Parliament to represent East Wolverhampton, the bitter truth had dawned on him: "The power of the Liberal Party was sinking."[41]

In fact, it had sunk. And that, by his own reckoning, was the great tragedy of Geoffrey Mander's political career. He had hitched his wagon to a flickering star. If they ever really had, people simply no longer seemed to be voting on the basis of Liberal principles but on the basis of more rationally calculated interests. Supporting either the Labour or Conservative parties was simply a more practical way of getting what one wanted than voting for a Liberal party that had never firmly or monolithically supported one class grouping against another.

Mander had joined the Liberals precisely because he thought they represented principles and not interests. But for a variety of reasons, he felt that principles were becoming increasingly less important in British politics, naked and unapologetically practical interests increasingly more so. There were sixty Liberal M.P.s in 1929, and the Labour government, lacking an independent majority, relied on them for support. This, Mander knew, was "the Party's last chance historically to be a parliamentary force," and to reverse the alarming trend. But he also knew that "the Liberal Party had never recovered from the disastrous split between Mr. Asquith and Lloyd George during the First World War."[42]

Mander had long lusted for a Parliamentary career, and it hadn't been easy getting there. But when he finally arrived, the Liberal harness he wore consigned him to the back benches. The aging radical clearly felt his ineffectualness very acutely. His unpublished autobiography (pointedly titled *A Back-Bencher Looks Back*) consists of one long, rather sad denial that he had been totally inconsequential in national affairs. The book was written, its author claimed, to show that the House of Commons was not run by whips alone, that a back-bench M.P. could still intervene effectively in the formation of policy. "He can do it by Parliamentary questions," Mander insisted, "by adjournment motions, by private members' bills, in addition to general debate and in other ways."[43]

Examples follow. In August of 1939, Home Secretary Sir Samuel Hoare decided that "The Link," an Anglo-German organization, was a Nazi propaganda agency. Hoare asked Mander to question him about it in debate, so the Home Secretary could reveal that he knew its true nature but was powerless to act until it broke the law. Mander complied.[44]

Equally dramatic demonstrations of Mander's contribution to national policy occurred in the area of private members' bills. Annually, he proposed a works' councils bill, which would have legislated the enforcement of labor-management consultation on certain industrial issues. Annually, the bill was defeated because the Ministry of Labour (never a Liberal portfolio) had to present its own schemes. Nevertheless, Mander felt "the point was made."[45]

Mander's back-bench activities made points to the public as well as to the politicians. In 1939 he introduced a conscription of wealth bill to enable the government "to call up wealth as well as lives" for the war effort. His colleagues laughed, but Mander knew no M.P. would vote against it for fear of his constituents' disapproval. He believed the British electorate learned something about its representatives when, to prevent the bill's coming to a vote, it was buried in committee.[46]

Needless to say, there were numerous parliamentary debates and committee activities in which Mander and other Liberals' influence on governmental action was of similar magnitude.[47] But Mander felt that, productive as it was, his career as a Liberal back-bencher left something to be desired. His constituents agreed. In 1945 he was defeated by a Labour candidate in East Wolverhampton. In 1948 he finally chose to break out of the Liberal straitjacket, and bolted his old party for Labour. Addressing himself to former associates, he explained that radicalism simply could not be effectively practiced by the Liberals in modern Britain, that a new grouping now represented (actually had been representing for some time) his ideology to the nation. "All the evidence goes to show," he declared, "that the Liberal Party has no future as a major parliamentary force." Reminding colleagues that "it is the things that are done that matter, not the name of the party that does them," Mander explained his switch by arguing that "the Labour Party is today the heir of the radical tradition." He observed that state ownership of coal, railways, and electricity had been advocated by the Liberals in their 1945 manifesto. But it was Labour that had achieved them, along with the National Health Service, the National Assistance Act, and the National Educational Act. He had finally decided to play on the side that would "GET THINGS DONE!"[48]

But time had run out for Geoffrey Mander. He was never returned to Parliament, although he did serve as a Labour member of the Staffordshire County Council for Brierly Hills. In addition to local affairs, he interested himself in promoting the League of Nations to the British public. The old radical, whose principles had transcended his own class location only to be contained by the realities of party politics, died in 1962. He had joined the Society for Psychical Research in 1905, and remained a member until just before his death. The National Trust's biographical pamphlet on him explicitly notes his faithful attendance at S.P.R. meetings.

Personality and Rationalization

An appraisal of these men might begin by noting the common characteristics that *cannot* be found, although they could have been expected to appear among aficionados of psychical research. It is really not too surprising that none of these men except Norris can be linked in any way to Spiritualism—and he in a highly distinctive way, emphasizing the spirits' transmission of genius to living individuals. Psychical research was simply not Spiritualism. For the same reason, it is not too surprising that except for Scott-Gatty none became affiliated with the S.P.R. during advanced age, when death often becomes an overriding consideration. What is fairly surprising is the paucity of evidence permitting even the suggestion that these were men imbued with a special intellectual concern for either religion or science. What is genuinely striking is the lack of evidence suggesting that they were particularly concerned with the conventional social referents of either religion or science (groups, institutions, practices).

Scott-Gatty's family background was clerical, Mander was for a while a member of the Modern Churchman's Union (although he doesn't even mention it in his own autobiography). Aside from that, their own presentations of their lives contain no mention of religious institutions or behavior, much less of religious thought. Regarding science, only Norris seems to have known much of it (unless we call Edge's technological skills, such as they were, evidence of scientific sophistication). Actually, only Norris seems to have had any contact with or even any particular interest in scientific institutions, scientists as a social group, or the social implications of formal, scientific thought in any sense. Of course, they all may have been both religiously and scientifically aware in ways the evidence doesn't show. But on the basis of the available material, there seems to have been no really extraordinary concern with either science or religion on an intellectual level. And, excepting Norris, there seems to have been no major concern with the institutions, groups, or processes most obviously representing either science or religion in society.

Yet each of these men affiliated himself in a substantial way with an organization offering an affirmation of "the soul" specifically as a "scientifically" defensible entity. If most were neither extraordinarily concerned with science nor extraordinarily concerned with religion, then why did they have such an affinity for an idea that was (in its own fashioners' view) explicitly a scientific-cum-religious statement? What might have been the pressures that sharpened these men's receptivity toward the secular soul? What were the common experiential referents?

With all due allowance for limitations in the available material on these men (especially Scott-Gatty), the following possibility can be suggested. Perhaps where the intellectuals in the S.P.R. had seen the soul, these men saw personality. Perhaps where the psychical researchers themselves had seen Science, these men saw bureaucratization, commercialization, routinization. Perhaps they saw the process of rationalization, embodied in certain organizational structures, as a threat to the expression of their own personalities.

Each does appear to have seen and to some degree resented the fact that his own particular field of activity was organized on the basis of practical, mundane goals and not on the basis of his own personal imperatives. In fact, each appears to have seen his own life as one long struggle to operationalize those imperatives in an indifferent or even hostile environment. According to what these men tell us of themselves, each felt his deepest, most innate qualities to be somehow constrained or even violated by the immediate social milieu within which he operated. Scott-Gatty's art, Cowan's martial spirit, Norris' genius, Manders' sociopolitical nobility, Edge's vision and adventurousness—had to struggle for expression within (and against), respectively, the music industry, the organized military, the scientific professions, the party system, and the entrepreneurial and general social climate.

These were not quietly functional men, who simply learned what was required to reap traditional social benefits (wealth, status, power) and then performed it. To gain those sorts of benefits, Edge could have entered the Army, or remained a successful bicycle company executive. Instead, he pursued a particularly dangerous career in a particularly tenuous industry. Mander could have enjoyed a life of leisure-class privilege or opted for a political career as a Conservative. He did not. Norris could have adapted his findings to the prevailing context of blood research, as others proved able to do, or at least at some point made some concession to his critics' views. Instead, he insisted on asserting his own genius. Cowan could have stayed in his own service during the Boer War, kept his mouth shut about Kronstadt, and sat out World War II. He would not. Scott-Gatty could have treated "the Professional world" not as some distinct environment hostile to art, but as a quite natural and necessary structure for its economic remuneration. He does not appear to have done so.

Each seems to have felt somehow chafed. And each seems to have insisted to the end on the primacy of innate qualities or personality over the forces that would canalize them. Perhaps excepting Norris—and, to a lesser degree, Mander—their complaint was not, as it seems to be of most complaining members of society, that the rewards of wealth, status, and power were not forthcoming in sufficient quantity. It was rather that the organization of their world was such as to provide insufficient amplitude for the expression of their own innate characters.

This is most emphatically not to suggest that any of these men was characterized by any blithe disregard for wealth, status, power, or any other tangible personal reward (any more than it has ever been suggested that psychical research in any sense dominated their lives). It is rather to suggest that the question of how their personalities were to find full expression in the social world was a serious, indeed a major and life-long, concern. Where Sidgwick, Myers, and others had seen materialism arraigned against metaphysics, these men seem to have seen certain institutional and economic structures arraigned not so much against their interests as against themselves. Where the psychical researchers had seen science versus the soul, these men seem to have seen rationalized social organization versus personality.

If that was the case, their apparent endorsement of the secular soul is not surprising at all. Other devotees of psychical research seem to have perceived much the same sociocultural issue, from somewhat more expansive perspectives.

MEMBERS: "THE OPERATIVE FORCE"

John Harris

John Harris' concern with the relationship between structural social arrangements and the potentialities of individuals living within them became acute in Africa. The relationship he recorded there was stark, and horrifying. In Africa, Harris found a situation in which the former quite rationally, quite methodically, and quite literally exterminated the latter.[49]

Harris' social background is not entirely clear, although he was born at Wantage, Berkshire, in 1874 and educated both privately and at King Alfred's School. His own wife said, "Of his family I knew but little, and my husband was never communicative and not at all interested in genealogies."[50] He came to London in 1890 as an apprentice in a London warehouse, and for the next seven years held some unspecified post in "a London commercial firm."[51]

But commerce was never Harris' forte. Along with an entire group of "ardent young Evangelicals engaged in business houses in the City of London" he supported a plan in Dr. F. B. Meyer's Baptist church to send one of their number to Africa as a missionary.[52] When funds were finally raised, it was Harris who was chosen to go. In the missionary training college that he attended prior to departure he met Alice Seeley, daughter of a Liberal, nonconformist temperance advocate "in the Silk Trade." They were married on the steamer that transported the missionary party up the Congo River.

Harris' recollections of travel in the Congo basin make colorful reading. But neither the crocodile and raw monkey meat meals, nor the encounters with scorpions and hippo herds, provided any preparation for the horrors that awaited him when he entered the Congo Free State. For the next fifteen years, Harris was to be immersed in a nightmare that might have robbed most people of any conception they ever held of the innate dignity of man.

His first revelation of what was actually happening there came when he found on his veranda the freshly severed hand and feet of a young African girl. They had been surreptitiously deposited there by her father in the hope that they might underscore to the new Christian missionary the disparity between his teachings and the conduct of the Congo's European taskmasters.[53] Harris learned very quickly that the girl's experience was hardly an isolated case. For the next few months he quietly sought out and photographed African atrocity victims while going about his teaching and medical work with the natives.[54]

Actually, Harris was already planning the course that would lead to the eventual overhaul of the Congo Free State. The fact that he was to succeed was in no small measure due to his intellectual appraisal of the situation. For what is so interesting about Harris is that, intellectually, he did not view what was happening in the Congo in terms of moral absolutes (i.e., the rape of innocent Africa by satanic whites). Consequently, he never dissipated his own reform energies in ineffectual howls of moral indignation (a route other missionaries had already taken). What Harris coolly surveyed and carefully documented was perhaps more terrifying than any such assessment could have been. He saw an entire economic system functioning, with perfect logic and impeccable efficiency, on the basis of monstrous first principles.

The principles were straightforward. First, the Congo Free State, with all its vast reserves of rubber, ivory, and gums, belonged to King Leopold of Belgium, personally. Second, the King's state had first claim on all native labor (as opposed to such tribal commercial arrangements as had existed for centuries). Third, the concessionaire companies of the state held as their sole priority in exploiting that labor the accumulation of the maximum amount of profitable materiel as quickly as possible. Informed by such superbly clear directives, the agents of the Congo Free State could and did construct a brilliantly functional administrative system. In fact, what most appalled Harris was its machinelike precision.

> The *machine* was surely the most devilish ever invented. Its starting point was that the negro "only respects the law of force and knows no other persuasion than terror," therefore, "terror" must be used to drive the rubbergatherers into the forests to work; next, that in exercising such terror, the rubber agents must always hit the workers where they would feel that terror most. Here, in short compass, is the admitted Machinery:
>
> 1. Seize from each village the old men, the women, the girls and the children. Hold them until the tale of rubber is complete to redeem them.
> 2. The seizing of these hostages to be carried out by armed native "Sentinels" (overseers). If there is hostility to them, then shoot.
> 3. The supply of cartridges to be strictly controlled by the white men in charge of the rubber collecting posts. As one check upon useless expenditure of cartridges, each Sentinel must bring in the hand or feet of the person he has killed.
> 4. In order to encourage the White Agents to secure an increasing quantity of rubber and ivory, each white man to be paid a bonus on the quantity secured.[55]

Harris found that in the storming of villages to take hostages, "the Sentinels often shot and missed, then fearing the consequences of insufficient tallies would perforce chop the hand or feet of a captive to make up the tally." He also saw "the foul and reeking hostage houses

. . . so horrible that no white man would willingly go near them," where "many hundreds of thousands died."[56]

But the enemy, to him, was not the corrupt, inmost recesses of white Europe's heart. It was "the machine": a rationally calculated system of commercial exploitation, principally of rubber, that quite deliberately exterminated thousands of Africans. And what is truly singular about Harris is that, moralist and missionary that he was, he insisted on applying his sociological analysis of this genocidal machine even to its own murderous operatives.

> The system was so vicious that within my knowledge I had never known an ordinary white agent who had been able to escape from its toils except by death. First, every white man arrived in debt to the Concessionaire Companies for passage and outfit; secondly, that even if he could liquidate his debt within a year and free himself, he was then liable to arrest and imprisonment for "irregularities" committed in his "area," of which, owing to early ignorance of the language, he probably knew nothing. The choice before such men was (a) to continue to operate the system they loathed; or (b) to resign and risk being put in prison, which in that climate meant certain death; or (c) to commit suicide. Many took the third alternative.[57]

And as rubber profits (ironically, probably the same rubber Selwyn Edge coveted for his motorcars) had generated the machine, so did rubber profits protect it.

> The new sense of comfort which rubber had given to travel, rubber dividends which were being paid up to 225% and even higher, were so widely spread in the U.S.A., Belgium, Holland, France, Germany, and Britain that together they acted as a deadly soporific to any threatened outburst of indignation.[58]

Harris knew he was up against harsh, tangible economic and political realities. But he was not about to allow any system or machine to prevent the expression of his own inner imperatives. And he was not entirely without resources. In secret, he and some clerical colleagues began informing influential men in England of what was happening in the Congo Free State, and petitioned them to instigate an inquiry. For the next six years he stayed in the Congo, conducting this clandestine campaign to force an external revision of the Congo Free State's system of exploitation. He sent his photographs to Lord Edmund Fitzmaurice, who passed them on to Lord Lansdowne. Lansdowne was an associate of E. D. Morel and was active in the Anti-Slavery Society. Through his and that organization's agitation an international commission of inquiry was established in 1906 to look into the missionaries' allegations. It consisted of a Belgian, President Dr. Edward Janssens; an Italian, Baron Nisco; and a Swiss jurist, M. de Schumacher. Harris heard of its coming "with unbounded joy," and began collecting witnesses. But the real struggle was just beginning.

Naturally, the local rubber supervisors made life as difficult as possible for Harris and his friends. They intimidated the missionaries and threatened the African witnesses with reprisals if they should testify to the commission. The men who stood to lose the most were the heads of King Leopold's concessionaire companies, represented in Harris' district by one M. Longtains.

But the terror campaign failed, and Longtains was called to account before the commission. To Harris, Longtains' testimony was the most dramatic incident of the entire affair.

> "I do not deny the charges," he said. The Commissioners were aghast.
> "I cannot deny the charges. I can explain the system."
> The explanation of M. Longtains was in fact absolutely accurate, namely, that the system under which the rubber was extracted with the aid of armed native sentinels capturing hostages could not fail to lead to outrages, and he produced a list of Sentinels killed when getting the rubber quotas.[59]

Longtains later escaped and fled, but Harris thought the tide had turned. "When the Commission left," he said, "the uppermost thought in the minds of all was that the King of the Congo Free State would

issue the Report without delay, and that a new era had dawned."
Actually, the struggle was far from over.

The commission's report was published but without the support-
ive testimony Harris and his associates had gathered. As time went on,
and there was no change in conditions, the Harrises decided to take the
battle home to England. With Morel, they formed the Congo Reform
Association, lobbying for the position that Britain and the other powers
had the right to intervene on the basis of the Anglo-Congo Agreement
of 1884 and the Berlin Conference of 1884–85.

In fact, there was a grotesque logic underlying Leopold's whole
administration of the Congo. Enormous and immediate profits were
required because the king's expenditures in creating a commercial
infrastructure (steamers, roads, stations, anti-slave-trade campaigns)
had been far in excess of expectations.[60] But when Lord Curzon and the
British Foreign Office decided that conditions in the Congo were having a destabilizing effect on neighboring Sudan, the monarch's position
weakened. It deteriorated further as British and other European re-
formers nurtured an indigenous Belgian opposition to the King's personal rule in the Congo. In 1908, Leopold was forced to surrender
responsibility for the area to the government and people of Belgium.

Harris, however, was not finished with the question of de-
humanizing social systems. The Congo Reform Association's goal had
been only the replacement of Leopold's personal rule, but Harris knew
the problem went far deeper. He almost seems to have felt that in the
Congo he had witnessed in microcosmic form the nightmarish potential of commercial civilization ("how little we realized the *debasing*
power of unbridled acquisitiveness"[61]). He spent the rest of his life
campaigning for the replacement of the very idea of commercial exploitation in any form with the concept of trusteeship as the rationale for
European rule in Africa and elsewhere in the nonwhite world.[62] He
became the major figure and eventual president of the Anti-Slavery and
Aborigine Protection Society, from which platform he fought any and
all attempts to reduce non-Europeans to the status of a labor market in

European-owned commercial ventures. He briefly held a Liberal seat in Parliament (1923–24), but the greatest triumph of his life came in 1932, when the League of Nations accepted the principle of trusteeship as a guideline for European government in colonial possessions. In 1933 he was knighted.

Harris died in early May of 1940. *The Friend,* a Quaker publication, noted in its obituary that his knowledge of West African trading conditions alone, to say nothing of his various other areas of expertise, would have enabled him to earn a large income in any number of ways.

But he never enjoyed one. Again and again, his entire life expressed the conviction that allegiance to commercial, and sometimes even national, interests was the surest means of destroying anything laudable within men. He had resisted "the machine"—the social, economic, and political systems that made fodder of human lives—to the best of his ability from the time he left the City of London until his death. He was a member of the Society for Psychical Research from 1901 until 1920.

Sydney Olivier

In an address to the Church Congress at Southampton on October 3, 1913, Sydney Olivier explained his view of what the concept of the soul meant to the world:

> It is our authority for revolt against the dogmatic fatalisms of hereditarians, Determinists, Eugenists; it is essentially individual, personal, free; and yet, far more certainly than any other touch of nature, its consciousness makes all men kin.[63]

Of course, the soul Olivier referred to was of a rather special sort. He described his personal estimation of it in a letter to H. G. Wells on September 27, 1917.

> I perceive . . . a continuity of my own personality, subsisting in relations perceptibly indestructible either in time or space, and unaffected by either, and of whose persistence after dissolution of my body I

have as little doubt as I have of their existence and their operative power in this life—they have been the *most* operative things in it for me—the rest of my activity is chemical or animal energy.[64]

Some "operative force" in Olivier did indeed provide authority for revolt against all dogmatic fatalisms. This remarkable man, bourgeois to his fingertips by choice as well as by birth, nevertheless spent a lifetime in revolt: against specific institutions, against social systems, against certain conceptions of history itself. G. B. Shaw described him as "a law unto himself."[65]

He was born on April 16, 1859, at Colchester, to wealthy parents. His father, Reverend Arnold Olivier, was curate of several parishes and a man of considerable means. Olivier said that the comfortable, genteel surroundings of his boyhood made him take for granted the external world, and enabled him to create a richly textured "private world" in which reposed all that he found most valuable. In a discussion of the effects of an adolescent love affair, he revealed something of what that private world provided.

> What it said to me was—Yes, you were right, she belongs; her being also is of the things that appear without observation, that lie beyond the web of the visible world and are known independently of its intelligence.
>
> Moreover, it revealed me to myself for a moment as exempt from exclusiveness and free . . . it was only in the flash of the first illumination of my recovered mystical world that I saw and understood my freedom.[66]

Freedom was important for Olivier. One of the first intellectual acts of consequence that he undertook was freeing himself from the world of orthodox religion, steeped in it as he had been from birth. By 1884 his attitude was such that he could write in these terms to his fiancée of a service he had attended in Whitechapel:

> I liked the service but it distressed me . . . because here was the universal language, music, beautifully rendered, to a scanty congrega-

tion, in a district of London to all appearance utterly dead and hopeless in most respects, and giving itself in all earnestness to forms which never-more, it seems to me, having lost as they have their hold on the hearts of the many and the intellects of the thinkers, can supply what is wanted for these people.

It seemed like some madness, the eternal "truth" of music, and the strength which simple bare expression in adequate language of conviction really felt gives to poetry, chained to this corpse.[67]

By that time, Olivier had almost absentmindedly slipped into what would become a highly colorful career in the foreign service. He had been educated at Tonbridge School and Oxford, where he became a close friend of Graham Wallas. Having prepared for no specific career, he decided in 1881 to take the civil service examination and, scoring well, was placed in the West Indies Office as a clerk. In London he met the Webbs and George Bernard Shaw, and began grappling with the great questions of social organization. Olivier considered himself a positivist at the time, and wrote to his fiancée of certain practical benefits he saw in socialism from that point of view (primarily the reduction of wasteful competition among capitalists).

But the same letter revealed an inability to choose between "Comte's ideal capitalist system or a socialist system of industry as most desirable" because both "postulate such an advance in our morality that one can scarcely judge by reasoning from present materials which would work best." The ability of a social system to provide adequate scope for the expression of personal moral values was always, for Olivier, the final criterion of its quality. He would not endorse socialism until he had satisfied himself that it held out the greater promise in that regard.[68]

When he had, however, he helped Shaw, Wallas, and the Webbs found the Fabian Society. But he made it clear that what attracted him to socialism was, specifically, its encouragement of individual morality—a quality he felt ascertainable in it on purely empirical grounds. In an essay on "The Moral Basis of Socialism," Olivier explained how, viewing morality from a positivist perspective (i.e., as the behavioral function of observable structural circumstances) he had determined that socialism was superior. Curiously, there was in Olivier's paper an explicit identification of morality with individualism. Society, he posited, exists to assist the individual in his struggles with nature; therefore, the best social structure was the one that enabled the individual to get the most victories from that range of interactions. At the same time, he defined morality as that which promotes social cohesion, immorality being that which sacrifices the common good to the private interest. By that reckoning, capitalism stood indicted as a system that was simultaneously immoral (because it gratified only the possessing classes at the expense of the commonwealth) and anti-individualistic (because far from abetting the individual's triumph over the forces of nature, it rendered him the mere plaything of market forces).

> Socialism appears as the offspring of Individualism, as the necessary condition for the approach of the Individualist ideal. . . . Socialism is merely Individualism rationalized, organized, clothed, and in its right mind.[69]

G. B. Shaw mischievously called Olivier's ideas "Schopenhauerian," but Olivier stood by his views. Ten years later, he was still defending his concern with the promotion of personalized, inner value systems, and the role that concern played in his own espousal of socialism: "I hold that the Socialist system will be more 'moral' than the present because the individual will get more freedom and satisfaction."[70]

The interesting thing about Olivier's perspective was its fundamental inability to endorse any analysis of social or even historical processes that sacrificed individual imperatives to the working out of some grand design. This was illustrated perfectly in a rather heated exchange between him and Shaw on the subject of the Boer War. Shaw, like many Fabians, had argued that the war was historically necessary, in a sense predetermined. Modernity, in the form of industrial capitalism, had to come to the Boers eventually, as it must to all sectors of the world community, in order that it might give birth and finally yield to socialism in the course of historical evolution. British imperialism in South Africa (motivated as it was by the exigencies of British capitalism) could only serve to bring the Boers a comparatively benevolent form of industrialism, from which they would eventually advance into the socialist garden history had so wisely planned for us all.

Olivier began his rebuttal of that position by denying that the Boer War (or, by implication, any war) was part of any cosmic scheme. The personal qualities (in this case, either the stupidity or the criminal egoism) of one man—Alfred, Viscount Milner—were, he argued, what made the difference.

> I am so far from accepting any fatalist position in either direction that when you argued the other evening that the Boers are a seventeenth century people and ———— that they are peasant proprietors and ———— that their industrial organization is condemned by the theories of their F.S. you all set my teeth on edge. . . . The analogous argument that the war was "inevitable" is equally impossible to me. . . . Of course, if Milner had not been such a BOOBY—which is the only possible term for him—there would have been no outbreak. But the whole course of events has turned on small divergences when one single man could have made all the difference. . . .
> *There would have been no war. There would have been a settlement.*[71]

Having expressed his opposition to the idea that the war should be countenanced as the logical outcome of great historical forces, Olivier then assailed Shaw's specific notion of British imperialism. Shaw considered it an ultimately progressive historical agent. But, argued Olivier, that was because Shaw knew nothing about it. Imperialism was what history was not: an engine, a machine, a system of power—the final effects of which depended entirely on the character of the men who made it run. Unhappily, those men were not as Shaw envisioned them.

> The Imperialist-Militarist movement . . . has *not* been a movement having for its aim the welfare of native races, still less the regulation of

capitalism in the interests of wage earners. . . . The recent surge has certainly been due to two things: one, a commercial self-interest (*not* a conscious imperialist force, but one using imperialism as its engine), and, two, an increasing addiction to a low form of stimulant, the excitement of militarism. . . . But the shoddy commercialism and the Kiplingite danger-drinking which has boomed us into our present position *do* imply that *in* the machine which has produced this state of things there are *not* imperialists of the type you would dream of—but only commercialists and swashbucklers—and you have the machine (commercial and military) beyond all record. . . . I confess that the South African wage-proletariat may go to the devil for me, and is likely to do so as long as the ———— profit engine follows its present odds. Make up your mind about Jamaica.[72]

This last remark referred to an impending trip to the West Indies that Shaw had been invited to join, and underscores the great paradox of Olivier's career. For Olivier was simultaneously an anti-imperialist Fabian socialist and a functioning component of the British imperial system. In 1891 he had been made principal clerk in the South African Department of the Colonial Office, where he had criticized both Cecil Rhodes' South African Chartered Company and the Home Government's failure to control it. He had felt it an entirely novel, and dangerous, state of affairs that traditional Colonial Office policies could be overridden, and perhaps in part for that reason found himself posted to a section of the empire yet untouched (unlike Africa) by the new breed of commercial-military expansionists mentioned in his letter to Shaw. In 1896 he served as acting secretary to the Sugar Commission in the West Indies, and in 1900 became acting governor of Jamaica.

It was in Jamaica that Olivier found his niche. He administered the island in 1902 and again in 1904, after it had been devastated by hurricanes in 1903. After a three-year spell in London as principal clerk for the West Indies, his prior record in Jamaica recommended him for a full term as governor when the island once more experienced extensive hurricane damage in 1907. Olivier held the post from 1907 to 1913. During that time he oversaw the reclamation of swamp lands, the rebuilding of roads, and the reconstruction of Kingston.

Olivier took a real interest in both his recovery work and in the history of Jamaica. He became particularly intrigued by the history of slavery. In fact, that was the specific subject of his speech at the Southampton Church Congress in 1913, in which he had referred to the soul as the authority for revolt against all dogmatisms and fatalisms. In the same address he again expressed his conviction that it was not the functionings of all-encompassing systems but the personal, moral choices of individuals that ultimately made history.

> Historians of civilization will demonstrate that the abolition of slavery and the extension of civic equality, education, and justice were economic and automatic necessities, and part of a general world-process. They did not so appear to either party concerned with them. They saw them brought about by the vehement agitation of men who held very definite convictions as to the nature of man and the principles on which negroes ought to be dealt with: principles condemned by sober practical men on the spot as fanatical and insane and certain to bring destruction upon Society.[73]

Olivier's career in the civil service was a successful one. In 1913 he became secretary to the Board of Agriculture; in 1917, he was assistant comptroller and auditor of the Exchequer. In 1924 Ramsay Macdonald made him secretary of state for India. However, throughout his career Olivier continued turning out books on conditions in the colonies—always with a pronounced anticapitalist thrust.[74] He never deviated from the position that it is not the system, imperial or otherwise, that makes the man. It is the man who makes the system.

Olivier had first joined the Society for Psychical Research in 1905. He was so active in it that in 1907 he was coopted as a council member, a position he was forced to decline only because of his appointment in Jamaica.[75]

Values versus Systems

Harris and Olivier are distinguished from the earlier group of S.P.R. members in two areas. First, they both came from religious backgrounds (even though only Harris made any public commitment to a church, and his was dispersed among several). Perhaps their respective religious backgrounds help account for the specific set of principles each espoused ("liberal-humanitarian" for Harris; "socialist-cum-individualist," in a striking combination, for Olivier). Those principles seem to have been the basis on which these men structured their entire lives.

In addition, these men are differentiated from the earlier contingent of S.P.R. members in that there was a greater breadth to each's vision of the world. Norris, Edge, and the others had been concerned primarily with their own particular areas of activity. Harris and Olivier each placed his own life in the context of a considerably larger social environment (Africa, the Empire, and so forth). For them, personal social values may have been the referent of "the soul." The referent of "science" may actually have been the systemization of social, political, and economic life along what they seem to have felt were, to say the very least, stiflingly utilitarian or narrowly materialistic lines.

These men resisted, considerably more sharply and actively than most of the others, the construction of "systems" within which each's principles were either irrelevant or downright dysfunctional. Their activism may have reflected their broader view of the systems enclosing them. Major efforts were demanded when the problem entailed, as it did in Harris' explicit view, nothing less than an entire structure of commercial exploitation. Machinelike and dispassionate in its daily operations, that structure almost seems to have struck Harris as hell bureaucratized—even when the overt atrocities of King Leopold's reign in the Congo were ended. It summoned from him a lifetime of opposition, however consequential the results. Olivier saw threats of even greater scope to his highly individualized moralism. He found danger in modern imperialism and in the industrial capitalism he felt it carried. He also found danger in the socialist alternative to industrial capitalism, even in history itself as some thinkers portrayed it. All imperiled his "operative force." All provoked his resistance in response. It surely seems more than coincidental that Olivier, the most radically "antisystem" of all the S.P.R. members discussed, was also the most deeply involved in psychical research. The further the mechanistic systems closed in, the more seriously his (or, by implication, anyone's) personal vitalism was circumscribed, the more cudgels he took up in opposition.

PSYCHICAL RESEARCH AND
MIDDLE-CLASS SOCIETY

From what is known of the lives of these seven devotees of the secular soul, it is now possible to propose the following tentative hypothesis. Psychical research and the notion of the secular soul probably provided intellectual support for people who found cause for alarm in the sociocultural processes of bureaucratization, routinization, and rationalization. It probably had an appeal or a public among the middle and upper classes to the degree that those processes were perceived as problems. That is, the secular soul was rather warmly received among the middle and upper classes insofar as the rational (i.e., goal- and not value-oriented) organizational structures of mass society seemed to threaten individuals' sense of their own unique, personal worth, or even that of man in some more general way.

The evidence for this is admittedly limited. Nevertheless, that sort of "fit" between individuals' lives and Edwardian psychical research may seem more plausible if another, closer look is taken at what the secular soul really was. For the striking irony of the situation is that precisely by trying so hard to be "rational" and "scientific," the psychical researchers had presented for public consumption practically the most nonrational version of human personality imaginable.

The secular soul was basically an expression of the bare essentials of the religious understanding of life as it had evolved in the West: the notion that individuals carry something ineffable within themselves, that the significance of man is not merely that accruing to any functioning component of a larger system (i.e., the material world) but rather that of an entity composed of distinct and mysteriously nonreducible stuff. Myers' telepathic subliminal self was what was left of the religious perspective when all else—all specific normative strictures, all specific behavioral suasions, all specific social prescriptions—had been stripped away. It embodied the position, advanced by theology from the beginning, that man is in and of himself cosmically significant. But unlike theology, it offered no means of understanding why or, more importantly, what was to be done about it. Psychical research had streamlined religion down to its core because its originators (especially Sidgwick) had felt religion could no longer be supported intellectually except perhaps on this, to them its last line of defense.

Psychical researchers had seen science as a way of viewing the world that denied or rendered meaningless the very notion of the miraculous, and feared it might eventually deny or render meaningless the idea that human existence was itself a form of miracle. Rather than attacking the scientific world view (as they saw it), they had tried to accommodate it. They yielded, like the Spiritualists, to the idea that what is meaningful is what is empirically known or knowable. They further yielded, unlike the Spiritualists, to the idea that what is meaningful is what is known about *this* world. They would yield all else, but they would not yield the soul. The Spiritualists had drawn their defense on the soul as well, but they had still linked the soul to the survival of death. Since survival was an entirely "other-worldly" and hence "unscientific" consideration to the psychical researchers, they had for all practical purposes jettisoned it along with all else (God, dogma, creed, church) that they thought unsound in scientific terms. Finally, they wound up barricaded before the idea that human personality is actually numinous in this world, in this life. Their telepathic subliminal self was the imagery of that idea.

It is hardly surprising, then, that they might have attracted individuals who felt the idea of personal, individual worth or even the value of personality in the abstract should be most strongly affirmed. By the Edwardian era, psychical research offered little else. The secular soul was neither more nor less than a celebration of nonmaterial individual personality simply because, like Everest, it was there. That was why the S.P.R. could attract both a Cowan and a Mander. There was simply nothing more to the Society than a celebration of personal essence for its own sake. What could be less "rational" a view of human personality?

But if the hypothesis proposed is at all tenable, then the question becomes: how strong and unqualified an affirmation of the value of personality or personal worth could modern, middle- and upper-class British society afford? How tolerant could society be of what psychical researchers, for want of anything else to say that would be "scientific," were screaming? Was the social world really organized, either structurally or culturally, to assimilate psychical research's version of selfhood? *Could* it be?

Actually, British society was presented with an alternative version of human personality, one that it would find far more acceptable than the secular soul. In fact, that alternative version was being elaborated at the same time that the individuals discussed here were affiliating themselves with the S.P.R. The Society's leaders were aware of it even then, in the early 1900s. What they didn't know, however, was that that alternative version of personality would eventually check them and what they stood for.

Its architect was Sigmund Freud.

NOTES

1. The fellows of the Royal Society were A. R. Wallace, Couch Adams, Lord Rayleigh, Oliver Lodge, A. Macalister, J. Venn, Balfour Stewart, and J. J. Thompson.

2. Cited by F. W. H. Myers in an obituary on Gladstone in the *Journal of the Society for Psychical Research,* vol. 8 (1897–98), p.260 (hereafter cited as *Journal*).

3. The names of all members of the S.P.R. were usually printed in the bound volumes of the *Proceedings* and the *Journal*.

4. Council meeting, March 12, 1897; Minute 9.

5. Some biographical material on Scott-Gatty can be found in *Grove's Dictionary of Music and Musicians,* 5th ed. (London: Macmillan, 1954) and in *Who Was Who,* vol. 2, 1916–1928 (London: A. and C. Black, 1967).

6. Scott-Gatty bequeathed a "Musical Diary and Ledger" to the Bodleian Library at Oxford (shelfmark ms. Eng. misc. b.81). It contains a record of all his professional output until his retirement in 1895. (This material is used by permission of the Curators of the Bodleian Library.)

7. S. F. Edge, *My Motoring Reminiscences* (London: G. T. Foulis, 1934).

8. R. S. Lyons, *Sir Malcolm Campbell's Book of Famous Motorists,* ed. Malcolm Campbell (London and Glasgow: Blackie and Son, n.d.), pp. 27–28.

9. Ibid., pp. 28–35.

10. A contemporary said this was the most striking thing about Edge in comparison to other motoring pioneers. Edge was "a world-famous motorist for whom mechanical things meant nothing at all and had no attraction. . . . Edge never had that love for mechanics which has shown itself at an early age in most of those who have earned world fame in the motoring world. What he learned about mechanical matters in later life was the outcome of necessity— he had no natural bent" (ibid., pp. 25–26).

11. Edge, *Reminiscences,* p. 7.

12. Ibid., pp. 205–27.

13. Ibid., pp. 177–90.

14. Ibid., p. 165.

15. The Veterans Car Club in Ashwell, Hertfordshire, has numerous newspaper clippings of Edge's activities, as well as one of the few available copies of his book.

16. *Autocar,* November 3, 1933.

17. Reported in the *Lancashire Daily Post,* February 20, 1934.

18. The title of Cowan's proposed book was "The Wheel of Fortune Through Seventy Years." A rough draft of this book is in the library of the National Maritime Museum in Greenwich. (This material is used by permission of the Trustees of the National Maritime Museum.)

19. In addition to "The Wheel of Fortune Through Seventy Years," there is a manuscript entitled "Portion of a Draft of Proposed Book Dealing with Matters which May Require Scrutiny by the Admiralty." It is apparently another draft, containing slightly different material, of the same book. Whether it is an earlier or later version is not known.

20. Cowan, "Portion of Draft," p. 46.

21. Ibid., pp. 50–51.

22. Ibid., p. 52.

23. Cowan, "Wheel of Fortune," p. 5.

24. Cowan, "Portion of Draft," p. 300.

25. A friend of a friend requested Cowan's restationing to his former post (Cowan, "Wheel of Fortune," p. 26).

26. Cowan, "Portion of Draft," pp. 175–220.

27. Ibid., p. 278.

28. Ibid., p. 320.

29. Norris is credited with the invention of a dry collodion photographic plate that is still used in spectrum analysis. His correspondence, and related manuscripts, are preserved in the library of the University of Birmingham. (This material is used by permission of the library of the University of Birmingham.)

30. Norris' account of the entire affair is contained in an undated letter to John Gamgee (Folder 161, Norris Collection, University of Birmingham).

31. This is the closing remark in the same letter to Gamgee.

32. On July 16, 1890, he wrote to Norris: "There are Baronets and Fellows of the Royal Society who were at the University College with my brother Sampson and myself, who can have no claim above us to such distinction but for the accident of wealth and social circumstances and to the success of cliques." He had earlier compared his own oppression to that of Galileo (March 31, 1890) (Folder 194, Norris collection).

33. Letter from Gamgee to Norris, July 16, 1890.

34. Ibid.

35. Letter from Gamgee to Norris, July 24, 1890.

36. Folder 129, Norris Collection, p. 18.

37. "An Inquiry Into the Laws Which Govern Spirit Intercourse With Man," Folder 129, Norris Collection.

38. Taken from *Geoffrey Le Mesurier Mander—Donor of the House*. This biographical pamphlet, published when Mander donated his home, Wightwick Manor, to the National Trust in 1939 (he was the first person to donate a home while still alive), is one source of information about Mander. More important ones, however, are the unpublished autobiography and miscellaneous writings housed in the library at the University of Bristol.

39. From a pamphlet written late in his career, *To Liberals* (pp. 5–6).

40. "A Back-Bencher Looks Back" (unpublished autobiography), p. 4.

41. Ibid., p. 15.

42. Ibid., p. 18.

43. Ibid., p. 1.

44. Ibid., p. 24.

45. Ibid., pp. 32–33.

46. Ibid., p. 30. Equally successful Mander measures were annual bills

to embody in British law the Covenant of the League of Nations, and efforts in 1933 and 1935 to set up an international police force.

47. Neville Chamberlain once scolded Mander for "liking to pose as the *enfant terrible* of the House" (ibid., p. 57).

48. From the pamphlet *To Liberals,* pp. 5–10.

49. Harris' manuscript collection is in the Rhodes House Library, Oxford. It consists of newspaper clippings, obituaries, and an incomplete biography composed of Harris and his wife's recollections of his life and career entitled "Sir John Harris."

50. "Sir John Harris," p. 5.

51. Obituary, *Christian World,* May 9, 1940.

52. Harris' personal religious convictions are as difficult to pin down as his social background. He was apparently born a Congregationalist (obituary, *The Wiltshire News,* May 8, 1940), but he represented a Baptist church in Africa, and later in his life became a Quaker. He is probably best described simply as a low-church Protestant Christian.

53. "Sir John Harris," pp. 37–38.

54. It is difficult to exaggerate the gruesome nature of these photographs.

55. "Sir John Harris," p. 43.

56. Ibid., pp. 43-44.

57. Ibid., p. 58.

58. Ibid., p. 37.

59. Ibid., pp. 56–57.

60. See Sydney Lew's articles in *The Times,* May 22 and 25, 1906.

61. "Sir John Harris," p. 61.

62. Harris said conditions in the Congo never really improved until this principle was adopted by Belgium in 1933.

63. *Sydney Olivier: Letters and Selected Writings,* ed. with a memoir by Margaret Olivier, with some impressions by Bernard Shaw (New York: Macmillan, 1948), pp. 193–94.

64. Ibid., p. 145.

65. Ibid., p. 9.

66. Ibid., p. 29.

67. Ibid., p. 62.

68. Olivier's original ambivalence on that score is revealed in a letter to his wife in 1884. Discussing Hyndman's *The Historical Basis of Socialism,* he complained that Hyndman "confines himself a good deal to showing the history of the growth of the Capitalist system, and its evils. What he does not do justice to, in my opinion, is the possibilities for good in that system, while

he ignores the inevitable evils of a Socialist system, organised without as thorough a revolution in morality as it would suffice to obviate the evils of the Capitalist system" (ibid., p. 64).

69. "The Moral Basis of Socialism," in *Fabian Essays in Socialism*, ed. G. B. Shaw (London: The Fabian Society, 1889).

70. Letter to Shaw, October 2, 1899. Olivier's correspondence with Shaw is housed in the Personal Manuscript Department of the British Museum.

71. Letter to Shaw, 1899 (no further date).

72. Letter to Shaw, 1899 (no further date).

73. *Sydney Olivier*, p. 191.

74. See his "The Economics of Coloured Labour," paper read to the National Liberal Club, 13 November 1906. Reprinted in "National Liberal Club, Political and Economic Circle," *Transactions*, vol. 5, pt. 12. See also *The Anatomy of African Misery* (London: The Hogarth Press, 1927).

75. His letter to the council was read, according to the Minutes, at its meeting of May 16, 1907.

Chapter Seven

The Eclipse of Psychical Research

FREUD, PSYCHOTHERAPEUTICS, AND THE DILEMMA OF PSYCHICAL RESEARCH

Some Edwardian S.P.R. workers seem to have felt that if psychical research were to be accepted as a science it would have to offer what science offered: practical benefits. There was within the S.P.R. an attempt to carry on the Myersian principle of relating psychical research to the general flow of developments in analytical psychology and psychotherapeutics.[1] In fact, it seemed for a while that Myers' ideas had placed them squarely in the middle of these new fields, if not in the vanguard. The Society for Psychical Research was attracting, as active investigators, people who had been impressed by Gurney and Myers' early delineations of the hypnotic trance state as a manifestation of the unconscious or subliminal personality. This group (Lloyd Tuckey, Milne Bramwell, V. J. Wooley, Constance Long, William Mac-Dougall, and others) was intent on developing the therapeutic applications of psychical research, specifically through hypnosis. Some were convinced that the concept of subliminal selfhood was a major step forward in the treatment of psychopathologies like multiple personality. One, T. W. Mitchell, has in his writings and his official work for the Society left an interesting record of what was actually British psychical research's attempt to cross an important threshold. Mitchell and the other medical men now affiliated with the S.P.R. were about to test the degree to which there was a practical, medical use for the secular soul.[2]

In 1912 they received authority from the council to establish a
medical section of the society, which was to publish at intervals special
sections in the *Proceedings* and in general abet the employment of
psychical research's findings in the treatment of mental disorders. But
there was another version of selfhood, as they came to realize, that
seemed more capable than their own of providing British culture with
what it needed.

Psychical researchers had of course been aware of Freud even
before Myers' death.[3] In the S.P.R. *Journal* for June 1910, Mitchell
noted that Freud's views were "arousing considerable interest" and
undertook a brief exposition of them for S.P.R. members by way of a
discussion of Ernest Jones' article in the April 15 issue of *The Psychological
Bulletin.* Mitchell acknowledged that "Freud's Psychology involves a
radical change in our attitude towards the questions of the structure
and functioning of the mind." Then, oddly, he implied that it was
nevertheless not as challenging to orthodoxy as the ramifications of
psychical research.

> The conception of the Unconscious (*Unbewusstsein*) as a sea of submerged
> ideas and emotions interacting with and determining the course of
> events in the consciousness which we know by introspection forms the
> foundation on which Freud's psychological superstructure rests. Freud's
> Unconscious is in truth not very different from Myers' Subliminal, but it
> seems to be more acceptable to the scientific world, in so far as it has
> been invoked to account for normal and abnormal phenomena only, and
> does not lay its supporters open to the implication of belief in supernor-
> mal happenings.[4]

Events would prove Mitchell correct, although he himself may
have misunderstood why. The entire response of the S.P.R.'s medical
corps to Freudian thought was curiously amorphous. They seem to
have recognized Freud's importance and even his accuracy in some
general way, yet they never formally conceded the implications his
ideas held for their own views. In November 1912, the S.P.R. *Proceedings* featured the first special section composed by the new medical

section of the Society. Produced under Mitchell's guidance, it consisted almost entirely of a discussion of the unconscious that reveals the basic inability of those who championed the secular soul to substantively relate their work to Freud's portrayal of mind and personality. It would appear that, at least in Mitchell's own case, the problem was essentially a nonintersection of vital interests. He saw something to celebrate; Freud saw something to cure.

Mitchell's paper "Some Types of Multiple Personality" turned out to be (after extended treatments of noteworthy clinical examples of the syndromes, particularly the Sally Beauchamp case) basically a rumination on the unitary source of the human personality.[5] His concluding remarks explicitly addressed themselves to Myers' argument that selfhood is essentially the experience, at any given time, of one out of a variety of forms of consciousness generated subliminally. To Myers, that subliminal storehouse had been the soul. And Mitchell's paper trundled along to a closing examination of that position in light of the facts of multiple personality. Could the subliminal region Myers had probed account for what was seen in this pathology? Mitchell decided that Myers' only error had been his reluctance to acknowledge the unitary nature of the subliminal ("there seems no reason why we should not regard one and the same soul as the effective ground in each and all of the phases of consciousness occurring in one individual"). But how then did that one soul produce so many expressions in the pathology of multiple personality, some of them overtly malicious? Mitchell submitted that in such cases the physical organism did not properly achieve that temporal progression of forms of consciousness that Myers would have considered normal life (i.e., the experience over time of varying expressions of the subliminal self, such as dreams, genius, inspiration, trance states, and so forth). Multiple personality was an example of the breakdown of whatever physical (neurological) screening mechanisms existed, so that two or more forms of consciousness actually battled for control of the organism at the same time. But Mitchell found nothing wrong with Myers' delineation of the subliminal as the repository of that which was marvelous in man. There was nothing, he insisted, to be feared in the human soul. Rather, there was a great deal to be feared when our physical systems betrayed it, when they somehow failed to deploy its facets properly and in sequence. In such cases, its true character was marred by the imperfect physical mechanisms with which it had to express itself. "One unitary soul may persist behind all dissociations of consciousness," opined Mitchell, "but it will be unable to appear as a unity, and its manifestations will be fragmentary and discordant. Its unity will be masked by the imperfections of its instrument."[6]

True to the tradition of psychical research, Mitchell had directed his energies toward an explication of the soul (which Myers had originally psychologized). In the following article, entitled "A Study in Hysteria and Multiple Personality, with Report of a Case," he described how one approached that unitary source of consciousness when it required adjustment, how one actually grappled with a malfunctioning secular soul. The paper is fascinating in its refusal to concede that expressions of the unconscious could reflect the unconscious' own deformities, in its insistence that only the mechanical dynamics of its expression marred its nature and required attention. Quoting Myers, Mitchell said of the progression of deviate personalities in cases of hysteria and multiple personality: " 'These are not pathological phenomena, but pathological revelations of normal phenomena, which is a very different thing.' "[7]

In his treatment of an afflicted girl, "Milly," Mitchell briefly used the technique of Freudian psychoanalysis. But he deliberately stopped short of its completion and reverted instead to hypnotic suggestion as the sole form of therapy. He suggested to the varying characters in Milly's personality that they do her no further harm, and they appear to have complied. Pointedly, Mitchell remarked: "Very likely from the Freudian point of view my analysis was incomplete, but I had attained my ends." He hadn't seen, or perhaps hadn't wanted to see, Milly's unconscious as something to be dragged into the light, there to dissipate as completely as possible whatever destructive energies it contained. And in this also he was true to the conceptual tradition of psychical research. The object of celebration simply could not be treated as if it were a cesspool. In all, Mitchell's work perfectly illustrates the conflicting pressures on psychical researchers attempting to demonstrate the therapeutic applications of their work while they tried to remain faithful to its basic *raison d'être*. How does one diagnose or treat deformations of personality without conceding anything ignoble in the unconscious components of selfhood? How does one doctor what one wants to venerate?

Freud himself (a corresponding member of the S.P.R.) had been asked to contribute an article to the medical section's "Special Medical Part" in the November 1912 issue of the *Proceedings*. His work opened on a stern, no-nonsense note, as if he were aware of lecturing the heirs of a rival tradition. "I wish to expound in a few words and as plainly as possible," he began, "what the term 'unconscious' has come to mean in Psycho-analysis and in Psycho-analysis alone."[8] His article went on to portray the unconscious as the repository of ideas that were strong but not acted upon. Hypnotic experiments, he submitted, torpedoed the argument that the unconscious consisted of latent ideas that when strong enough become conscious. Those Freud labeled the "foreconscious." In contrast, unconscious mental activity was expressly prohibited from reaching the level of consciousness, and in fact consisted of those ideas and impulses that had been deliberately rejected as unworthy of operationalization in normal, daily, conscious existence. He concluded by arguing that it was in dreams, where foreconscious and unconscious thoughts converged, that the structure and laws governing unconscious life could be discerned.

Freud did not go into detail when describing the character of that unconscious mental life, but his version was already well enough known. A brief allusion to the sense of revulsion patients felt when the unconscious was unveiled was revealing enough. ("Psycho-analysis leaves no room for doubt that the repulsion from unconscious ideas is only provoked by the tendencies embodied in their contents.") The difference between Freud's portrait of subliminal personality and Myers' was the difference between the River Styx and Elysian Fields. As if to compensate, the concluding article in the "Special Medical Part" offered Boris Sidis' objections to Freud's ideas. Sidis, while no Myersian, was at least not yet ready to acknowledge the accuracy of Freud's depiction of the unconscious as charnelhouse. ("The 'unconscious' brain-processes are problematic entities and there is no way of getting at them.")[9]

Mitchell and the British medical psychical researchers continued to deal with Freud in a gingerly fashion. They went on expressing admiration for his accomplishments,[10] but they never came out with an open discussion of the impact Freud had had on their own formulations. This refusal to confront the issue head on is rather strange, especially in light of Mitchell's declaration in 1939 that "the very foundations of medical psychology, on which we had built for over twenty years, had been shaken by the work of Professor Freud and his pupils."[11] In America, there were some at least who were trying to come to terms with the matter.

In 1914, Leonard Troland published a paper in *The Journal of Abnormal Psychology* entitled "The Freudian Psychology and Psychical Research." In it he briefly discussed Myers' notions of the subliminal, then flatly stated: "How different from this is the Freudian view, in which the subconscious appears to be composed of the moral and aesthetic excreta of the ideal life." He continued:

> The essential forces in subconscious activity are ordinarily those of lust and malicious envy. The Doctrine of "die Animalität des Unbewussten" throws a light upon subconscious phenomena which is quite different from that cast by the mere romantic theory of Myers. On the basis of the Freudian hypothesis we should expect that the most grossly immoral subconsciousnesses would be possessed by those persons who in their supraliminal activities are the most guileless; conscientious clergymen when under the influence of their suppressed complexes should exhibit highly villainous tendencies. On the other hand, rakes and cutthroats, when intoxicated or dreaming should be pure-minded and gentle. . . . If we accept the Freudian hypothesis with all its implications we must admit that the faculties of the subconscious mind are more commensu-

THE SECULAR SOUL VERSUS
THE PSYCHOANALYTIC MODEL
IN MODERN, MASS SOCIETY

to avoid the suspicion that there is some strange connec-
the waning of psychical research's core formulations and
Freud's in twentieth-century British and American cul-
the period between the two world wars, when Freud's
sexuality seemed so novel, he was often seen as a cultural
a great liberator of the irrational, instinctive part of men
culture had repressed. Alongside that, psychical research
emed to embody a quaintly retrograde ethos. If compari-
le, it would have been thought to represent the naive, the
nd Freud the new, the emancipating.

he century wore on, Freudian thought came to be under-
rent terms. With the appreciation of his work that genera-
sis (to say nothing of clinical experience) have brought, it
hear Freud described as a champion of the subconscious
e mapped, or indeed as a force for its "unleashing" in any
nse at all. His vision was, of course, far more complex
is concern was not with the emancipation but with the
e taming of that irrational part. His goal was to make his
see that the time-honored tactic of coping with the sub-
mple repression, couldn't work. A tragically naive denial
psychical realities, repression merely invited violent ex-
ead, Freud's therapeutic mode offered an honest acknowl-
subconscious energies and their subsequent application to
ble activities (i.e., the process of sublimation). He never
he basic requirements of any civilized social order.[17]

his is understood, it becomes tempting to suggest that
he secular soul and acceptance of the psychoanalytic model
reflect the same social realities. For, given certain features
ial organization, psychical research was dysfunctional in

rate with those of dumb animals than with the powers and limitations
which we ordinarily recognize as human.[12]

If Troland's article offered a reductionist version of Freudianism,
it was shamelessly inaccurate on psychical research. Like many in
America, he still saw the latter as "spiritism," pure and simple (most of
the article is devoted to the proposition that, on the basis of Freud's
insights, it is not possible to accept at face value anything said by
mediums or Spiritualists about anything). Hereward Carrington's rejoinder in the following issue of *The Journal of Abnormal Psychology*
naturally took pains to point out Troland's mistaken portrayal of the
field. He noted that "the majority of continental psychical researchers
do not accept the spiritistic hypothesis to account for the facts,"[13] and
then proceeded to criticize Troland's factual grasp of the material he
was discussing. Finally, however, he could not resist shifting his gaze
from Troland to make an orthodox psychical researcher's reply to
Freudianism.

> A word, finally, as to Dr. Troland's exposition of Freud's theory of the
> subconscious. . . . According to this theory, the best people would be
> the worst and *vice versa*. We "repress" what we will not have in the
> conscious mind; it goes into the subconscious. Good! The purest-
> minded man or woman, then—according to this doctrine—is not the
> one who had the purest conscious mind; but the purest subconscious
> mind—that is, one who has let out all the "bad" it contains and retained
> more. So that, the more vilely we act, the more foul-mouthed we are,
> the purer we are as a matter of fact. What a delightful doctrine! . . .
> Unless we bring the contents of the subconscious mind to light, as the
> Freudians do, we should never know that we had one. Yet according to
> them, this is the man—this muck heap—this is the real man![14]

Carrington's sputterings, while betraying little appreciation of
the complexity of Freudian thought, nevertheless reveal the visceral,
immediate reaction that champions of the secular soul must have felt
when confronting his doctrines. For the American had blurted out
what Mitchell and the British tried to tiptoe around. The Freudian

subconscious did stand in stark contrast to that of Myers; the inner depths of personality Freud saw did not remotely resemble the secular soul. Freud's inner man was not the source of joy and inspiration but of lust and mayhem. Deformed personalities, according to him, were not manifestations of the physical body's inability to channel properly the magnificent energies lying at the base of our being—they were manifestations of the mind's inability to control properly the potentially destructive forces that were, in fact, our selves. In this, the psychical researchers simply could not concur. But, whether they knew it or not, that was the model of selfhood with which they had to compete.

The S.P.R.'s medical section had a very short history, and its demise is an institutional reflection of psychical research's inability to meet that competition. During World War I, the medical section was discontinued because another organization was able to assume the task of applying psychological thought to therapeutic practice with more success. In 1905, the British Psychological Association had formed a Psycho-Medical Society (from an earlier Society for the Study of Suggestive Therapeutics) in London. During the war, that organization's members were active in treating cases of shell shock and other war-related neuroses. Experience in those areas revealed that Freudian concepts and modes of therapy yielded practical benefits in the process of rehabilitation. After the war, the British Psychological Association decided to form its own medical section to continue experimentation with such techniques, the organ of which was *The British Journal of Medical Psychology*. The S.P.R.'s medical section was simply left to wither.

What was happening, of course, was more serious than the folding of a special branch of the Society. Psychical research itself had reached a conceptual dead end. Unwilling or unable to entertain the notion that the subliminal self might not be an altogether delightful aspect of the human entity—that it was not, in a word, holy—the psychical researchers could only stand and watch as other investigators proceeded to supply what the surrounding culture seemed to want. Others were already trying to answer the questions psychical researchers

could not even ask: how to modify
psychical energies within the self.

Within the S.P.R., there woul
more attempts to apply findings to
Throughout the Edwardian era, the
would be only the same (by this tir
subliminal self did indeed exist a
people seemed to be listening. Th
winners and fellows of the Royal Sc
the S.P.R. There would be fewer a
even interested in psychical research
handful).[15] Slowly but surely, the c
the Myersian secular soul, was disso
discipline. And as commitment to
liminal selfhood faded, as that de
untenable (outside the psychical
Freud's, the entire discipline went

The new direction came from
prise had in a sense begun. In
University essentially dismissed th
for the field. He defined telepathy
stratum of personality but merely a
all the way back to square one: th
mediation by sensory channels. He
sychology," and concentrated on fi
ment that many scientists had in
beginning. Under his leadership,
periments on the newly named p
tion," including "clairvoyance" (
distance) and "psychokinesis" (dire
there had once been a whole sub
tion, an entire secular soul to
guessing experiments and attem
dice.[16] The central paradigm of th

It is di
tion be
the wa
ture. D
emphas
revoluti
that mc
must ha
sons we
reaction

Bu
stood in
tions of
is now r
personal
substanti
than tha
more effe
own cult
conscious
of unalter
plosions.
edgement
socially tc
lost sight

Whe
rejection c
of personal
of British

the key area where psychoanalysis was quite functional: the understanding individuals are to have of the proper deployment of their personalities in the world. The Myersian paradigm had offered precisely what was not tolerable to a mass society organized for functional efficiency; Freud offered precisely what was desirable. Just how badly out of synchronization the idea of the secular soul really was in modern Britain—quite apart from any consideration of the quality of evidence supporting it—is perhaps best understood by another look at its lay enthusiasts.

The seven individuals previously discussed apparently all confronted one basic question: the degree to which the professional, bureaucratic, and institutional structures that bounded bourgeois British life could permit the expression of inner, personal drives. These individuals felt those drives demanded expression. The antagonism they seem to have felt most acutely was that between their own sense of inner substance and the social structures set up to channel individual talents and energies into the world. The truth is, those structures were neither intrinsically encouraging nor intrinsically hostile toward the operationalization of personal drives. They were indifferent.

"The Professional world" (i.e., the publishing industry) that ensnared Scott-Gatty was no more engineered to injure the sensibilities of gifted artists than it was intended to gratify their keenest aesthetic impulses. It was designed to make the musical talents of the few available to the many (for the enrichment of some). The moguls of the bicycle and motorcar industries made their production decisions on the basis of cost accounting and market formulas, into which a racing daredevil's sense of the dramatic might or might not fit. The military was structured quite carefully to make selective, not indiscriminate, use of a warrior's energies. His talents were to be deployed on the basis of estimations of the nation's interests, not his own inclinations. Neither Huxley nor the Royal Society, it is now abundantly clear, had any particular desire to thwart recognition of Richard Norris' genius. That he could not achieve that recognition without them reflected the simple fact that mechanisms existed to process and screen scientific thought before it was presented to the public as truth (and that he *did* not achieve it reflected the fact that he was wrong, not that he had been singled out for persecution). If Parliament did not allow much scope for the expression of Geoffrey Mander's compassion, it was because its constellation of party forces did not exist to provide a power level for Geoffrey Mander but rather to provide political representation for the mass society on whose behalf it was supposed to legislate. The structures in which all these men operated were designed to service as effectively as possible that mass society's tastes and consumption patterns and to order and control its security, its storehouse of knowledge, and its public policies. That is, they were organizational particulars of a rationalized, mass society.

Harris and Olivier confronted different sorts of structures, but those structures were similarly constituted and these men made similar sorts of demands on them. They quarreled with the Empire on the grounds that it was not organized as an expression of their own personal values, as if it ever had been or could be. In fact, they actually quarreled with commercial systems as systems, both capitalist and socialist. Finally, Olivier went so far as to quarrel with the notion that history can be understood as "systematic" not just in a specific sense (e.g., the Marxian) but in any sense at all.

These individuals apparently found in modern social life cause for a curious form of terror: the anonymous functionalism of constituent components. What they seem to have wanted was not something easily provided by the systems serving and directing mass society on the basis of rational (i.e., functional) considerations. They wanted leeway for the expression of nonfunctional (e.g., Edge's daring) or even dysfunctional (e.g., Cowan's warmongering) qualities. Their radicalness, if such it be, derives from the fact that they demanded that expression in the public sphere—not the private. They were not content to seek recognition of inner substance among a few intimates, or to confine its cultivation to the realm of fantasy or devotional life. They actually wanted that recognition from their own day-to-day, working worlds. But that may be something no modern mass society can afford to offer individuals.

It is also something that is considered infantile in Freudian thought. In psychoanalytic terms, it can be called a failure to find socially acceptable ways of sublimating personal drives, a neurotic insistence that those drives take precedence over the realities of the world as it is. This is not to suggest that all the individuals treated here would be considered in desperate need of therapy by psychoanalysts (although some, like Norris and Cowan, and probably Edmund Gurney, actually might be). It is rather to suggest that all might be considered fundamentally naive regarding the world; fundamentally misinformed regarding their own true natures and those of others; fundamentally wrong in their expectations of which gratifications the world could or should offer individuals.

Those are, of course, the classic rationales for rejecting any ethos that is subversive to the existing social order. To the degree that the Freudian model was accepted, to the degree that its process of sublimation has been successfully prescribed, devotees of the secular soul could only lose their cultural battle. And, with the rejection of that alternative, the most fundamental organizational features of mass society could only grow stronger. Oddly, it may have been Myersian psychical research, not Freudianism, that was the more seriously subversive of what we call "modern" culture and social organization.[18]

If so, we might more seriously judge whether we approve or disapprove of this peculiar discipline, with all its things that go bump in the night.

No such judgment, of course, can be rendered here. For, ultimately, psychical research itself is not the real issue at all. Its story was, and still is, a story of needs: needs that were and are religiously derived, emotionally acute, but socially and culturally problematic. As long as there are places where people with a commitment to the ineffability of the individual must confront both a culture that questions the idea of ineffability and a social system that simply ignores it, those needs will remain. Whether they are among those that should or can be gratified is a matter for each of us to determine.

Notes

1. R. Laurence Moore's discussion of this process (in *In Search of White Crows*) submits that psychical research was never integrated into the main body of psychological learning in America largely because of the obtuseness of the director of the American S.P.R., James Hyslop. In the famous Doris Fischer case of multiple personality, Hyslop and Dr. Walter Franklin Prince argued that the "Sleeping Margaret" character's claim to be a spirit was in fact true, thus identifying American psychical research with its Spiritualist predecessor. The American approach to such matters might usefully be compared to the British, especially as presented in Mrs. Sidgwick's argument that mediumistic controls were essentially secondary personalities or impersonations at the hypnotic level of consciousness ("A Contribution to the Study of the Psychology of Mrs. Piper's Trance Phenomena," *Proceedings,* vol. 28, pp. i–xix, 1–652).

2. It is important to bear in mind that Mitchell and his colleagues never considered themselves mere agents for the reorganization of religious responses to personal problems. In a review of a book entitled *Religion and Medicine: The Moral Control of Nervous Disorders* (by Worcester, McComb, and Coriat), Mitchell expressed open hostility to any such scheme. "To make temporal well-being or welfare a motive for religious faith is to revert to a type of faith which all the higher religions of the world have already outgrown" (*Journal,* vol. 14 [1909–10], p. 104). The secular soul, to its devotees, was a *secular* soul.

3. Myers himself had considered Breuer and Freud's paper "The Psychical Mechanism of Hysterical Phenomena" to be a resounding confirmation of his own general linkage of hysteria to the uncharted regions of the subconscious rather than to the neurological system, *à la* Charcot. "I could not wish for a more emphatic support, from wide clinical experience, of the view of hysteria to which my own observations on different branches of automatism had already, by way of mere analogical reasoning, directed my thought" (quoted by T. W. Mitchell in "The Contributions of Psychical Research to Psychotherapeutics," *Proceedings,* vol. 45, pp. 175–86 (quote, p. 180).

4. *Journal,* vol. 14, p. 353.

5. *Proceedings,* vol. 26 (1912–13), pp. 257–85.

6. Ibid., p. 284.

7. Ibid., pp. 286–311 (quote, p. 286).

8. "A Note on the Unconscious in Psycho-Analysis," ibid., pp. 312–18. (quote, p. 312).

9. "The Theory of the Subconscious," ibid., pp. 319–43 (quote, p. 343).

10. A "Special Medical Supplement" of the July 1914 *Proceedings* carried an endorsement of Freud's ideas on dream formation by V. J. Woolley ("Some Auto-Suggested Visions as Illustrating Dream-Formation"), and an enthusiastic review of Freud's *Psychopathology of Everyday Life* by Constance Long. Long may have been getting uncomfortably close to the real implications of Freudian thought for the secular soul. "It is, indeed, easier to apply psychoanalysis to our neighbors than to ourselves," she said, "but what we discover in the psychology of another is rarely far from what is present in our own personality" (vol. 27 [1914–15], p. 414).

11. "The Contributions of Psychical Research to Psycho-therapeutics," *Proceedings,* vol. 45, pp. 182–83. Mitchell was referring specifically to the decline of interest among medical men in hypnotism as a therapeutic agent, and its replacement by psychoanalysis.

12. *The Journal of Abnormal Psychology,* vol. 8 (1913–14), pp. 408–10.

13. *The Journal of Abnormal Psychology,* vol. 9 (1914–15), p. 411.

14. Ibid., p. 415.

15. Aside from William MacDougall, Gardner Murphy and C. G. Jung were really the only major psychologists after Freud who interested themselves in psychical research. Within the intellectual community as a whole, Henri Bergson, C.D. Broad, F.C.S. Schiller, Gilbert Murray, and Arthur Koestler come to mind as perhaps its best-known supporters.

16. See R. Laurence Moore's *In Search of White Crows* for an excellent treatment of Rhine and the pressures under which he worked.

17. Probably no scholar has done more to explicate this aspect of Freudian thought for those outside as well as within the psychoanalytic profession than Philip Rieff, especially in *Freud: The Mind of the Moralist* (New York: Viking, 1959). It might be noted that Rieff's ten-volume *Collected Papers of Sigmund Freud* (New York: Collier Books, 1963) includes one volume entitled *Studies in Parapsychology.* In Freud's essays "The Uncanny" and "Dreams and Telepathy," contained in this volume, non-neurological mental phenomena are quite explicitly interpreted as manifestations of the individual's subconscious fears and desires, to be understood in terms of the Freudian delineation of the subconscious rather than the secular soul of the psychical researchers.

18. There is, of course, a continuing debate as to whether or not Freudian thought and practice contribute to the preservation of a given political and economic status quo. Carl Schorske, among others, argues that there is a "depoliticizing" element in Freud that helps perpetuate ongoing systems (see his "Politics and Patricide in Freud's 'Interpretation of Dreams'," *The American Historical Review,* vol. 78 [1973], pp. 328–47). On the other hand, the Frankfurt School of Marxist scholars has found in Freudianism grounds for indictments of capitalist society (see Marcuse's *Eros and Civilization,* or nearly anything by Erich Fromm). The point made here, however, regards not capitalist or socialist socioeconomic structures but the entire mode of social life we imply by the term "mass society."

Bibliography

Individual articles from the *Proceedings of the Society for Psychical Research, The Journal of the Society for Psychical Research, Light,* and, with a few exceptions, newspaper articles are not listed in this Bibliography.

PRIMARY SOURCES: PUBLISHED

Braid, James. *Magic, Witchcraft, Animal Magnetism, Hypnotism, and Electro-Biology.* Edinburgh: A. and C. Black, 1852

Capron, E. W. *Modern Spiritualism: Its Facts and Fanaticisms, Its Consistencies and Contradictions.* Boston: Bela Marsh, 1855.

[Carpenter, W. B.] "Spiritualism and Its Recent Converts." *Quarterly Review,* vol. 131 (October 1871), pp. 301–53.

Carrington, Hereward. "'Freudian Psychology and Psychical Research': A Rejoinder." *The Journal of Abnormal Psychology,* vol. 9 (1914–15), pp. 411–16.

Charcot, Jean-Martin. *Clinical Lectures.* London, 1887.

Crookes, William. *Researches in the Phenomena of Spiritualism.* London, 1874.

Crowe, Catherine. *The Night Side of Nature.* London, 1852.

Donkin, Horatio. "Mystery-Mongering." *The Saturday Review of Politics, Literature, Science and Art,* vol. 56 (August 4, 1883), pp. 595–96.

————. "On Thought-Reading." *The Nineteenth Century,* vol. 12 (July–December 1882), pp. 131–33.

Edge, Selwyn Francis. *My Motoring Reminiscences.* London: G. T. Foulis, 1934.

Edmonds, John Worth. *Spiritual Tracts.* New York: 1858.

Gillson, E. *Table-Talking: Disclosures of Satanic Wonders.* Bath, England, 1853.

Godfrey, N. S. *Table-Tilting Tested and Proved To Be the Result of Satanic Agency.* London, 1853.

Gurney, Edmund. "A Chapter on the Ethics of Pain." *Fortnightly Review,* vol. 36 (1881), pp. 778–96.

———. "An Epilogue on Vivisection." *Cornhill Magazine,* vol. 45 (1882), pp. 191–99.

———. "On the Nature of Evidence in Matters Extraordinary." *National Review,* vol. 4 (1884), pp. 472–91.

———. *The Power of Sound.* New York and London: Basic Books, 1966 (reprint of 1880 edition).

Gurney, Edmund, and F. W. H. Myers. "A Theory of Apparitions, Part II." *The Nineteenth Century,* vol. 15 (June 1884), pp. 791–815.

Gurney, Edmund, F. W. H. Myers, and Frank Podmore. *Phantasms of the Living.* 2 vols. London: The Society for Psychical Research and Trübner, 1886.

Hardinge-Britten, Emma. *Modern American Spiritualism.* New York: The National Spiritualist Association, 1870.

———. *Nineteenth Century Miracles.* New York, 1884.

Heidenhain, Rudolf. *Hypnotism or Animal Magnetism.* London, 1888 (reprint of German edition, 1880).

Home, Daniel Dunglas. *Incidents in My Life.* London, 1861.

———. *Lights and Shadows of Spiritualism.* London, 1890.

Huxley, Thomas. *Collected Essays.* New York: Appleton, 1894.

Liébeault, A. A. *Etude sur le zoomagnétisme.* Paris, 1883.

Light: A Journal of Psychical, Occult, and Mystical Research (London: Eclectic Publishing) 1881–1900 (published weekly).

London Dialectical Society. *Report on Spiritualism of the Committee of the London Dialectical Society.* London: Longmans, Green, Read, and Dyer, 1871.

Lyons, R. S. *Sir Malcolm Campbell's Book of Famous Motorists.* Edited by Malcolm Campbell. London and Glasgow: Blackie and Son, n.d.

Maudsley, Henry. *Natural Causes and Supernatural Seemings.* London: Kegan, Paul, Trench, 1886.

Morley, John. *The Struggle for National Education.* London: Chapman and Hall, 1873.

Myers, F. W. H. "Automatic Writing, or the Rationale of Planchette." *The Contemporary Review,* vol. 47 (1885), pp. 233–49.

———. *Fragments of Inner Life.* London: The Society for Psychical Research, 1961 (reprint of 1893 edition, privately published).

———. *Human Personality and Its Survival of Bodily Death.* 2 vols. London: Longmans, Green, 1903.

———. "Multiplex Personality." *The Nineteenth Century,* vol. 20 (November 1886), pp. 646–66.

"The National Importance of Research." *Westminster Review,* vol. 99 (1873), pp. 343–66.

Olivier, Sydney. *The Anatomy of African Misery.* London: The Hogarth Press, 1927.

————. "The Economics of Coloured Labour." Paper read to the National Liberal Club, November 13, 1906. Reprinted in "National Liberal Club Political and Economic Circle." *Transactions,* vol. 5, pt. 12.

————. "The Moral Basis of Socialism." In *Fabian Essays on Socialism,* edited by G. B. Shaw. London: The Fabian Society, 1889.

————. *Sydney Olivier: Letters and Selected Writings.* Edited with a memoir by Margaret Olivier, with some impressions by Bernard Shaw. New York: Macmillan, 1948.

Podmore, Frank. *Modern Spiritualism.* 2 vols. London: Methuen, 1902.

Romanes, George John. *A Candid Examination of Theism.* Boston: Houghton, Osgood, 1878.

Rymes, J. S. *Spirit Manifestations.* Boston, 1881.

Seybert Commission. *Preliminary Report of the Commission Appointed by the University of Pennsylvania to Investigate Modern Spiritualism.* Philadelphia: J. B. Lippincott, 1887.

Sidgwick, Henry. *The Methods of Ethics.* 7th ed. Chicago: University of Chicago Press, 1962.

Society for Psychical Research. *The Journal of the Society for Psychical Research.* London, 1884–1930.

————. *Proceedings of the Society for Psychical Research.* London, 1882–1940. The *Proceedings* were published by various firms during this period.

Stone, G. W. *An Exposition of Spirit Manifestations.* London, 1852.

The Times (London). June 30, 1853 (Faraday article); February 20, 1861 (Sidgwick letter); October 11, 1876 (Slade trial); August 2, 3, 5, 1892 (Congress of Experimental Psychology).

Troland, Leonard. "The Freudian Psychology and Psychical Research." *The Journal of Abnormal Psychology,* vol. 8 (1913–14), pp. 405–28.

Tyndall, John. *Fragments of Science.* 6th ed. New York: Appleton, 1892.

Webb, Beatrice. *My Apprenticeship.* London: Longmans, Green, 1926.

PRIMARY SOURCES: ARCHIVAL

Minutes of council meetings of the Society for Psychical Research. S.P.R. Archives, London.

Personal Manuscript Collections

Cowan, Sir Walter H. Drafts of unpublished autobiography, "The Wheel of Fortune Through Seventy Years" and "Portion of a Draft of Proposed Book Dealing with Matters which May Require Scrutiny by the Admiralty." Library of the National Maritime Museum, Greenwich. Correspondence with Admiralty figures. Personal Manuscript Department, British Museum, London.

Edge, Selwyn Francis. Assorted newspaper clippings, obituaries, and supplemental material. Veterans Car Club, Ashwell, Hertfordshire.

Harris, John. Incomplete biography entitled "Sir John Harris," and miscellaneous scrapbooks, correspondence, and newspaper clippings. Rhodes House Library, Oxford University.

Mander, Geoffrey Le Mesurier. Unpublished autobiography, "A Back-Bencher Looks Back," plus assorted political writings. Library of the University of Bristol.

Norris, Richard Henry. Collected papers. University of Birmingham.

Olivier, Sydney. Correspondence with G. B. Shaw. Personal Manuscript Department, British Museum, London.

Scott-Gatty, Alfred. "A Musical Diary and Ledger." Bodleian Library, Oxford University.

SECONDARY SOURCES

Altick, Richard D. *Victorian People and Ideas*. New York: World, 1964.

Arendt, Hannah. *Between Past and Future*. Cleveland: Meridian, 1963.

Baldwin, Mark. "The London Congress of Experimental Psychology." *The Nation,* vol. 55, no. 1419 (September 8, 1892), pp. 182–84.

Barr, Stringfellow. *The Pilgrimage of Western Man*. Philadelphia: J. B. Lippincott, 1962.

Barth, Karl. *Epistle to the Romans*. Translated by Edwyn C. Hoskyns. London: Oxford University Press, 1950.

Bellah, Robert. "Civil Religion in America." *Daedalus,* vol. 96 (1967), pp. 1–21.

Bendix, Reinhard. *Max Weber: An Intellectual Portrait*. New York: Doubleday, 1960.

Berger, Peter. *A Rumor of Angels*. Garden City, N.Y.: Anchor, 1970.

———. *The Sacred Canopy*. New York: Doubleday, 1967.

————. "A Sociological View of the Secularization of Theology." *Journal for the Scientific Study of Religion,* vol. 6 (Fall 1967), pp. 3–16.

Broad, C. D. *Religion, Philosophy, and Psychical Research.* New York: Harcourt, Brace, 1953.

Brown, Burton Gates. "Spiritualism in Nineteenth Century America." Ph.D. dissertation in history, Boston University, 1973.

Carrington, Hereward. *The Story of Psychic Science.* New York: Ives Washburn, 1931.

Cox, Harvey. *The Secular City.* New York: Macmillan, 1965.

Doyle, Sir Arthur Conan. *The History of Spiritualism.* London, 1926.

Durkheim, Emile. *The Elementary Forms of the Religious Life.* New York: Free Press, 1969.

Eiseley, Loren. "Alfred Russel Wallace." *Scientific American,* vol. 200, no. 2 (February 1959), pp. 70–84.

Eliade, Mircea. *Birth and Rebirth.* Translated by Willard Task. New York: Harper and Row, 1958.

Ellenberger, Henri. *The Discovery of the Unconscious.* New York: Basic Books, 1970.

Ellul, Jacques. *The New Demons.* New York: Seabury, 1975.

Gauld, Alan. *The Founders of Psychical Research.* New York: Schocken, 1968.

Geertz, Clifford. "Religion." *The International Encyclopedia of the Social Sciences.* New York: Macmillan, 1968.

George, Wilma. *Biologist Philosopher: A Study in the Life and Writings of Alfred Russel Wallace.* New York: Abelard-Schuman, 1964.

Gouldner, Charles. *The Coming Crisis of Western Sociology.* New York: Avon, 1970.

Grisewood, H., ed. *Ideas and Beliefs of the Victorians.* New York: E. P. Dutton, 1966.

Groethuysen, Bernard. "Secularism." *The Encyclopedia of the Social Sciences.* New York: Macmillan, 1934.

Hall, Trevor. *The Spiritualists.* London: Duckworth, 1962.

————. *The Strange Case of Edmund Gurney.* London: Duckworth, 1964.

Hansel, C. E. M. *ESP: A Scientific Evaluation.* New York: Scribner's, 1966.

Houghton, Walter. *The Victorian Frame of Mind, 1830–1870.* New Haven: Yale University Press, 1957.

Inglis, Brian. *Natural and Supernatural: A History of the Paranormal.* London: Hodder and Stoughton, 1977.

Kahler, Eric. *Man The Measure.* New York: Pantheon, 1943.

Kuhn, Thomas. "The History of Science." *The International Encyclopedia of the Social Sciences.* New York: Macmillan, 1968.

Le Bras, Gabriel. "Déchristianisation: mot fallacieux." *Social Compass,* vol. 10, no. 6 (1963), pp. 445–52.

Livingston, James C. *Modern Christian Thought.* New York: Macmillan, 1971.

Lukes, Steven. *Emile Durkheim.* Middlesex, England: Penguin, 1973.

Mackintosh, H. R. *Types of Modern Theology.* New York: Scribner's, 1937.

Macrae, Donald. *Max Weber.* New York: Viking, 1974.

Marcuse, Herbert. *Eros and Civilization.* New York: Vintage, 1962.

Martin, David. "Towards Eliminating the Concept of Secularization." In *Penguin Survey of the Social Sciences,* edited by Julius Gould. Baltimore: Penguin, 1965.

Mauskopf, Seymour, and Michael McVaugh. "J. B. Rhine's 'Extra-Sensory Perception' and Its Background in Psychical Research." *Isis,* vol. 67 (June 1976), pp. 161–89.

Merton, R. K. "Science, Technology, and Society in Seventeenth-Century England." *Osiris,* vol. 4 (1938), pp. 360–632.

Mitzman, Arthur. *The Iron Cage: An Historical Interpretation of Max Weber.* New York: Grosset, 1970.

Mommsen, Wolfgang J. *The Age of Bureaucracy: Perspectives on the Political Sociology of Max Weber.* New York: Harper and Row, 1974.

Moore, R. Laurence. *In Search of White Crows: Spiritualism, Parapsychology, and American Culture.* New York: Oxford University Press, 1977.

Murphy, Gardner. *The Challenge of Psychical Research.* New York: Harper and Row, 1961.

Nelson, G. K. *Spiritualism and Society.* New York: Schocken, 1969.

Otto, Rudolf. *The Idea of the Holy.* Translated by John W. Harvey. New York: Oxford University Press, 1958.

Parsons, Talcott. "Christianity." *The International Encyclopedia of the Social Sciences.* New York: Macmillan, 1968.

———. "Christianity and Modern Industrial Society." In *Theory, Values, and Sociocultural Change,* edited by A. Teryakian. New York: Harper, 1963.

———. *Essays on Sociological Theory.* New York: Free Press, 1954.

———. *The Structure of Social Action.* Glencoe, Ill.: Free Press, 1937.

Richet, Charles. *Thirty Years of Psychical Research.* New York: Macmillan, 1923.

Rieff, Philip. *Collected Papers of Sigmund Freud.* 10 vols. New York: Collier Books, 1963.

———. *Freud: The Mind of the Moralist.* New York: Viking, 1959.

Robertson, Roland. *The Sociological Interpretation of Religion.* New York: Schocken, 1970.

Rogo, D. Scott. *Parapsychology: A Century of Inquiry.* New York: Taplinger, 1975.

Sage, M. *Mrs. Piper and the Society for Psychical Research.* London: The Society for Psychical Research, 1903.

Salter, W. H. *The Society for Psychical Research.* London: The Society for Psychical Research, 1970.

Schorske, Carl. "Politics and Patricide in Freud's 'Interpretation of Dreams.'" *The American Historical Review,* vol. 78 (1973), pp. 328–47.

Shiner, Larry. "The Concept of Secularization in Empirical Research." *Journal for the Scientific Study of Religion,* vol. 6 (Fall 1967), pp. 207–20.

———. "Toward a Theology of Secularization." *The Journal of Religion,* vol. 45 (1965), pp. 279–95.

Sidgwick, Arthur and Eleanor. *Henry Sidgwick: A Memoir.* London: Macmillan, 1906.

Smith, Ronald G. *Secular Christianity.* New York: Harper and Row, 1967.

Turner, Frank Miller. *Between Science and Religion.* New Haven: Yale University Press, 1974.

Vahanian, Gabriel. *The Death of God.* New York: Braziller, 1961.

Weber, Max. *From Max Weber.* Edited by H. H. Gerth and C. Wright Mills. New York: Oxford University Press, 1946.

———. *The Protestant Ethic and the Spirit of Capitalism.* Translated by Talcott Parsons. New York: Scribner's, 1968.

———. *The Theory of Social and Economic Organization.* New York: Oxford University Press, 1947.

Index

Adams, Couch, as S.P.R. member, 154n
Altizer, Thomas J. J., and "Death of God" movement, 13n
America
    civic values in, 14n
    emergence of Spiritualism in, 1, 18–25, 35n–36n
    evangelical movements in, 13n
    investigation of Spiritualism in, 34n
    psychical research in, 70, 84n, 93, 97, 167, 172n
    reaction to Freud's ideas in, 164–65
American Society for Psychical Research, 70, 93, 95
Anglicanism, 3–5, 14n, 40
Apparitions, S.P.R. studies of, 69, 72–73, 91–93, 100
Arendt, Hannah, on religion and politics, 11n
Association for the Advancement of Science, 32–33, 39
Automatic writing, 72, 79

Bacon, Francis, and religious tradition, 26
Balfour, Arthur, as S.P.R. member and Sidgwick student, 42, 109

Balfour, Eleanor. See Sidgwick, Eleanor
Baptist sects, 4
Barnum, P. T., as exhibitor of mediums, 19
Barrett, William
    in America, 70
    and criticism of S.P.R., 79–81
    and founding of S.P.R., 38–39, 41
    work of, on thought reading, 39, 43–44, 57, 61, 94
Barth, Karl, as conservative, 12n
Bellah, Robert, and American "civil religion," 14n
Berger, Peter, and Catholic concept of divinity, 11n–12n
Bernheim, Hippolyte (physician at Nancy clinic), 68
Binet, Alfred, and attack on hypnotism, 88
Blackburn, Douglas, and Brighton mesmerist, 63–64
Blavatsky, Madame, and Theosophical movement, 70, 86n
Bonhoefer, Dietrich, and liberal tradition, 12n–13n
Braid, James, and study of trances, 67
Bramwell, Milne, and research on hypnosis, 159

1 2 3 4 5 6 7 8 9 10 11 12 13   90 89 88 87 86 85 84 83 82